THE USBORNE BOOK OF THE
HAUNTED WORLD

Caroline Young
Designed by Stephen Wright
Illustrated by Graham Humphreys

Consultant: Tim Dedopulos BSC
Edited by Cheryl Evans

Additional help: designs, Andrew Dixon; typesetting,
John Russell; editorial, Helen Edom and Rachael Swann

Contents

What is the supernatural?

Most people have heard stories about ghosts. If you look up the words 'ghost', 'phantom' or 'spirit' in a dictionary, it usually says something like 'the reappearance of someone that is dead'. That's a very simple definition for an incredibly varied phenomenon that appears in different forms all over the world. As well as stories about ghosts and haunted places, which change and grow in the telling, there are thousands of reports of other spooky happenings world wide. These things often cannot be explained in terms that we usually use to understand our experiences; they form part of another world, the realm of the supernatural, meaning things that are 'outside nature'. This map shows some of the world's supernatural mysteries; many more lie on the pages ahead. Whether you believe in them or not is entirely up to you...

True or false?

All over the world, scientists and other experts try to prove or disprove supernatural happenings. For instance, societies of ghost hunters strive to prove that ghosts really do exist by painstaking investigation. Ghost hunters prepare a 'haunted' site, sealing draughty doors and windows and sprinkling dust around to show up any tiny movement. Some use machines to show any changes in temperature, and sensitive sound-recording equipment. Often, absolutely nothing happens. But some ghost hunters have succeeded in taking photographs of ghosts. Many such pictures can be explained away, but some have defied the scientists' tests. What do you make of these two photographs?

This machine was designed to record spirit voices.

This shadowy figure was caught on film in Raynham Hall, England, on September 16, 1935.

This is Lord Combermere, photographed in his chair as his funeral was taking place.

© Fortean Picture Library

© Peter Underwood FRSA

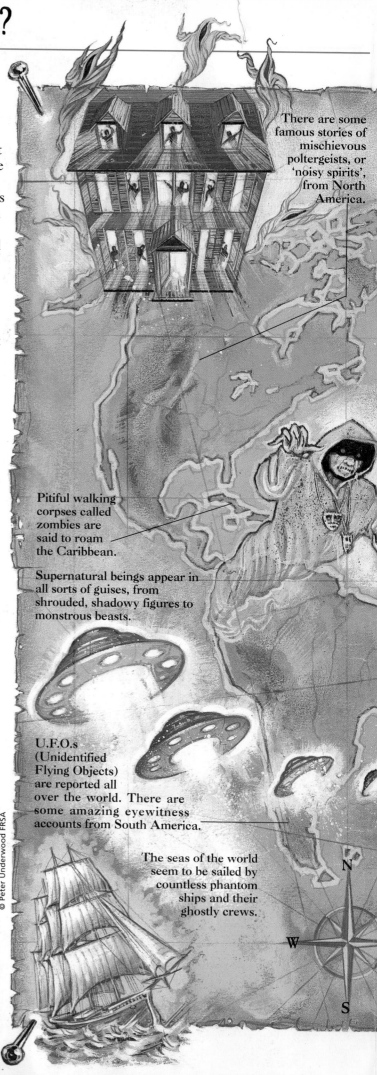

There are some famous stories of mischievous poltergeists, or 'noisy spirits', from North America.

Pitiful walking corpses called zombies are said to roam the Caribbean.

Supernatural beings appear in all sorts of guises, from shrouded, shadowy figures to monstrous beasts.

U.F.O.s (Unidentified Flying Objects) are reported all over the world. There are some amazing eyewitness accounts from South America.

The seas of the world seem to be sailed by countless phantom ships and their ghostly crews.

N
W
S

Britain seems packed with haunted spots. Most old buildings are reputedly visited by ghosts in some form.

Ancient legends describe the seas around Scandinavia as hiding huge serpents called Lindorns.

Chilling stories of fierce, blood-sucking vampires are often told in the countries of Eastern Europe.

Japanese ghost stories can be vivid and violent, telling of spirits keen to take revenge on their enemies.

In China, hideous walking corpses seem to feature in many traditionally-told ghost stories.

Magical spirits called genies fill the pages of many stories from the Middle East. Some are good, some wicked.

In India and Tibet, some people can learn to use amazing supernatural powers, it seems.

In Africa, witch doctors strive to drive out evil spirits with a variety of traditional cures.

The Great Pyramids of Egypt may hide many unsolved supernatural mysteries and unexplained powers.

Ghostly warnings and strange curses are at the heart of spooky stories from Australia and New Zealand.

Haunted houses

The best time to be in a haunted house is at night. Then, strange sounds echo down corridors, phantom figures walk through walls and lights go out without warning. Some buildings seem to bear the scars of violent scenes that have taken place in them. They are haunted by the sad, restless ghosts of people who suffered there.

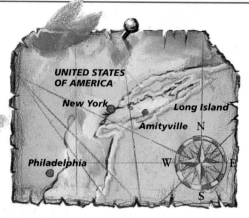

Hoax or horror?

One of the most famous modern haunted houses is in Amityville, near New York. It was here that Ronald DeFeo murdered six members of his family in November, 1973.

When the Lutz family moved into the stylish house shortly after Ronald's imprisonment, they were delighted with their new home. After an unforgettable month, the terrified family fled Amityville forever.

Night terrors

Ronald DeFeo shot his parents, two brothers and two sisters at 3.15 am. At that exact time every night, the Lutzes said the house filled with eerie noises. Windows and doors opened on their own, red eyes glowed in the darkness and prints of huge, cloven hooves appeared in the snow outside. When green slime began oozing down the walls and black syrupy stuff seeped through the keyholes, the Lutz family moved out.

A famous fake?

There is no doubt that the Lutzes made lots of money from the story of their brief time in Amityville. Experts now think it may all have been a hoax, but the tale is still a gripping one.

Ruthless revenge

A less famous, but grander, home is the ruined castle in Clisson, in northern France. It is haunted by the ghost of a widow, Jeanne de Clisson.

On August 2, 1313, Jeanne's husband Count Olivier de Clisson was beheaded as a traitor by order of King Phillippe IV.

The Count's widow, Jeanne, left her castle at Clisson to live in a poor fisherman's hut with her two young sons. She was plotting a terrible revenge on the king.

The castle at Clisson once towered above the town. Today, it is in ruins.

Ships of death

Jeanne equipped three warships with black-painted hulls and blood-red sails. With herself as their admiral, Jeanne led these ships in a thirteen year campaign to destroy the king's ships, killing any nobles and courtiers she found on board herself. She always left a few sailors alive on each ship, to tell the king about her. As the years passed, King Philippe and his family were struck by tragedy. By 1328, he and all his sons were dead, so Jeanne ended her campaign. Her sons returned to Clisson, but Jeanne vanished. Her sad spirit still stands on the ruined battlements of her former home, they say, gazing out to sea.

Faces in the floor

Unfortunately for one woman, the ghosts in a cottage in the Spanish village of Belmez refused to vanish. Her troubles began in August 1971. As she was cooking in her kitchen, her grandchild pointed at the ground.

Staring up from the tiles covering the floor was a face, its eyes wide with terror and pain.

Hidden horrors

The old woman scrubbed the floor and even had it dug up and replaced with concrete, but more anguished faces appeared. Over the next two years, eighteen faces were seen. Officials discovered that the cottage had been built on an old graveyard and said that the faces might belong to the dead who were buried beneath the floor.

Just as experts had 'bugged' every room with microphones, the weird phenomenon stopped. The ghastly faces have never reappeared...yet.

Tower of death

The gloomy Tower of London, overlooking the Thames, has witnessed thousands of horrible deaths over the centuries. With such a gruesome history, it's not surprising that the ghosts of those who died there stalk the Tower's grim rooms from time to time.

Fallen heroes

In the 1500s, Sir Walter Raleigh spent thirteen years in one of its damp cells, waiting for execution. His ghost is still seen, apparently, pacing back and forth in his cell.

Guy Fawkes, leader of a failed plot to blow up Parliament on November 5th 1605, was tortured and executed in the Tower. The building is said to resound with his screams on certain nights of the year.

Guy Fawkes led a large gang of conspirators.

Fated queen

Henry VIII ordered his second wife, Anne Boleyn, to be beheaded in the Tower in 1536 because she had not given him the son he so desperately wanted. Her white-robed ghost has been spotted in the Tower many times, sometimes with, sometimes without, her head.

In 1864, a terrified guard ran his bayonet right through the phantom queen when she walked through a thick wooden door in front of him.

Foul murders

Probably the most famous spooks in the Tower are the princes, Edward, who was twelve years old, and his brother Richard, who was ten. As heirs to the English throne, many rivals wished them dead. Imprisoned in the Tower, the princes were murdered in 1483. Their killer was never found, but many suspected the princes' uncle, Richard, who became king after their deaths.

In 1674, some builders found a chest containing two boys' skeletons. The bones were properly buried and the little princes' spirits vanished.

More houses

Houses have a past, just as people do. The ghosts of people who once lived in them are sometimes so attached to a house for some reason that they cannot leave it, but continue to haunt it long after their death.

Borley Rectory

Borley Rectory was once called 'The most haunted house in England'. It stood on a lonely spot in Suffolk, southern England, but was destroyed by fire in February 1939. The strange happenings at the Rectory had fascinated ghost experts for years, making it famous worldwide.

People who lived in the Rectory told of a phantom nun peering through their windows. A path in the garden became known as the Nun's Walk, as her lonely figure, dressed in a flowing, black robe, was often seen scurrying along here with her head bent low. Nobody knows why she haunts the Rectory, though some say she was punished for trying to elope with a monk by being shut in a room in the Rectory to starve to death.

Who is the phantom nun seeking inside the Rectory?

Several occupants of Borley reported seeing a phantom black coach pulled by two horses speeding silently through the Rectory gates. Others spoke of having stones thrown at their windows and hearing ghostly bell-ringing, strange noises and phantom footsteps in the house.

This plan shows the house and grounds of Borley Rectory.

Borley Place · Black coach pulled by two horses seen here. · Summer house · Rectory · Nun's walk

An expert investigates

In 1937, a ghost expert named Harry Price rented the Rectory for a year. His team of investigators noted every noise and strange happening during their tenancy. Although Price's book about Borley, *The Most Haunted House in England*, became famous, some experts said that he had faked a lot of the evidence in it.

Even though only ruins of Borley Rectory remain today, people still visit it in the hope of a glimpse of a ghostly nun or a spectral coach.

Ghostly guests

Glamis Castle in Scotland is a famous ghostly haunt. A drunken earl is said to play cards with the Devil in a sealed room there. Some tell of a monstrous baby that lived for centuries hidden from the world by its shamed family.

KEY:
1 Glamis, Scotland
2 Bisham Abbey and Borley Rectory, England
3 Blandy, France

Many French castles are haunted. At Blandy, near Paris, spooks fly around the chateau every year on November 1st. A former lord of the castle has also been seen, dressed for battle and riding a white horse.

Bald ghost · Devil's cards · Tragic nun · PACIFIC OCEAN · CANADA Toronto · San José · Rifle house · Closet death · Flying spooks · JAPAN · Tokyo · Haunted pond · ATLANTIC OCEAN · INDIAN OCEAN

William Lyon Mackenzie was the first mayor of Toronto, Canada. He died in 1861, but still haunts his former house. He was bald, so he wore a wig. Reports speak of a 'little bald man in a frock coat' roaming the house.

Apparently, a violent murder took place in a Tokyo house. The victim's head was thrown into the garden pond and his screams haunted the house. Peace only returned when the pond was emptied and the victim's skull properly buried.

In the 1500s, Dame Elizabeth Hoby locked her young son William in a closet in Bisham Abbey to finish his studies; but she forgot about him, and the boy died. The ghost of his mother still grieves through the gardens.

House of the spirits

Sara Winchester came from the wealthy American Winchester family, who made rifles. When her husband died, she said that spirits had told her to build a home for the ghosts of the thousands of people killed by Winchester rifles. Only by doing this would she avoid their curse.

© San Jose Convention & Visitors Bureau / Winchester Mystery House

Amazing maze

Building the 'home for ghosts' in San José, California went on seven days a week for thirty years. Sara Winchester kept changing her mind about what she wanted as she said the spirits' building instructions altered. Hidden by thick trees, the enormous house grew and grew. Inside, it was like a maze. Staircases went nowhere, doors opened into thin air and rooms were walled shut. Sara's spirit advisers seemed fond of the number thirteen, too. The house had to have thirteen bathrooms, stairways had thirteen steps, and each glittering chandelier had thirteen lights.

Lonely banquets

Mrs. Winchester lived a strange life in her haunted house. She held grand banquets for her ghostly guests, but she was the only diner servants saw. Each night, she locked herself into a tiny room dressed in a flowing blue robe and held secret 'meetings' with the spirits. She slept in a different bedroom every night and never had any visitors.

Today, the Winchester Mystery House is a big tourist attraction. However strange it seems, something very powerful drove Mrs. Winchester to build the house, whether it was madnesss, or ghostly orders, nobody will ever know.

Haunted isles

Swathed in mist and steeped in history, the castles and stately houses of the British Isles are home to hundreds of ghosts. Many other old buildings boast of being haunted by at least one former inhabitant, too. A popular theme in British ghost stories seems to be a hidden crime that comes to light in the spookiest of ways. Here are two chilling examples of such tales.

Murder

In one old story from Banffshire in Scotland, a pedlar called at a large country house with a bagful of beautiful fabrics to sell. The lady of the house ordered her servants to chase him off her land.

Unfortunately, events turned violent and the poor pedlar was murdered in the fight. The servants quickly hid his body and took his bag of goods to the lady. Horrified, she vowed to tell her husband of the crime and to punish the servants.

Fatal greed

But once she saw his purse full of gold coins, and the gorgeous green cloth in his bag,

greed overcame her good intentions. She hid the coins behind a tapestry in her room and had a beautiful dress made from the shimmering green cloth. She said nothing to her husband about the unfortunate pedlar, or his death.

Green ghoul

Some years later, the lady died, but she continued to haunt her family, unable to find peace in the grave. One night, her ghost appeared to the family nurse, dressed in the green dress she had made from the dead pedlar's cloth.

Sobbing as she spoke, she confessed her guilty secret and begged the nurse to let everyone know what had happened to the innocent man. She told the nurse to lift the heavy tapestry. When she did, there lay the stolen gold coins. The nurse then told the lord exactly what had happened on that fateful day years earlier. The Green Lady was never seen again.

Strange prisoner

A concealed crime also haunted a stately home called Nannau, near Dolgellau in Wales. In 1402, a nobleman called Owain Glyndwr visited Hywel Sele, the lord of Nannau, to ask him for support in fighting King Henry IV of England. The two men walked off into the gardens, talking excitedly. Later, Glyndwr left Nannau in great haste.

Sele did not return to the house and was never seen again.

For forty years, Nannau was haunted by the tormented ghost of its lost lord. One night, as a terrible storm raged, a bolt of lighting tore open the trunk of an old oak tree. Imagine the servants' horror as they saw a skeleton wearing clothes belonging to their former lord hidden inside the tree's trunk, suddenly lit up by lightning. Glyndwr, disappointed at Sele's lack of support for his battle plan, had murdered him and hidden his body in the hollow tree. Once released from its cramped prison, the ghost of the murdered lord left Nannau in peace.

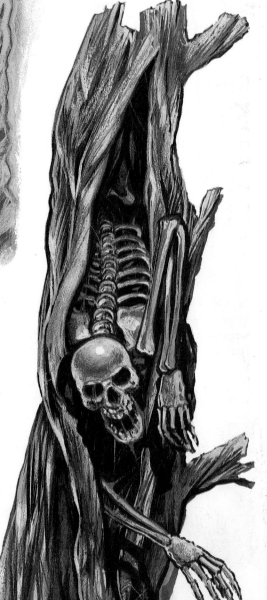

Sele's tell-tale skeleton emerged from a hollow oak tree during a thunder storm.

8

Unseen murder

Murder is always a terrible crime, but murder of a baby is perhaps worst of all. This famous story begins one rainy night in 1575, near Hungerford in southern England. As the local midwife was going to bed, she heard a carriage stop outside. Opening the door, she was surprised to see a servant from nearby Littlecote House, home of William Darrell. Darrell was known as 'Wild William' for his reckless habits and cruelty. The servant told the midwife that she was needed at Littlecote House because a woman was having a baby. The midwife gathered her things, but was shocked to be forced to wear a blindfold all the way to the room where the woman lay.

Vital clues

The midwife delivered the baby, but no sooner had she wrapped it in a blanket than someone grabbed it from her. The horrified midwife then heard the baby being thrown into the roaring fire. A purse of coins was thrust into her hands and someone roughly pushed her out of the room. As she left, she snipped some curtain material from the bedroom. She also counted the stairs as she was hurried down them into a carriage. The next day, the midwife reported what had happened to the magistrate. Investigations matched the material to a bedroom in Littlecote House and the number of stairs as leading to a particular room. The baby's mother was a maid who was seduced by Darrell. Fearing discovery, he had murdered it as soon as it was born.

Justice

Although 'Wild William' managed to bribe his way out of punishment at his trial, he paid for his awful crime fourteen years later. His horse reared and Darrell fell and broke his neck. People said the ghost of his murdered baby had terrified the wicked villain's horse.

Screams and wails

Farther south, in the village of Bettiscombe, another angry ghost made life miserable around 300 years ago. Crops withered in the fields and farm animals suddenly died. Worst of all, the air was filled with terrible, bloodcurdling screams every night. They seemed to come from one grave in the village graveyard.

buried in the village graveyard. Only when his bones were dug up and his skull hidden in the manor house did the screaming and the bad luck stop.

Apparently, the skull is still kept in Bettiscombe Manor.

Broken promise

In one version of this story, the grave belonged to a slave of the family who lived in Bettiscombe Manor. He had come to England with his master from the West Indies and had begged to be buried in his homeland when he died. His master had promised faithfully to carry out this request, but he died before the slave and nobody else paid any attention to the slave's wishes. When the time came, he was

Time to die

Heart-wrenching weeping, howling and screaming keep people awake in Ireland, according to long tradition. The source of this unbearable noise is a spirit called a banshee, who usually comes to warn them that one of their family is going to die. Most banshees look like women, though they may be young or old. Some look grotesque, with one nostril, one tooth that sticks out and webbed feet.

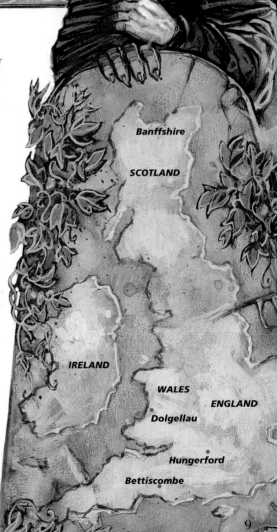

Banffshire

SCOTLAND

IRELAND

WALES

ENGLAND

Dolgellau

Hungerford

Bettiscombe

Phantom animals

Animals can become ghosts, too, if you believe the many stories about phantom animals. Some of these tales are about much-loved dead pets haunting their owners. Others, which describe strange, dangerous animals with a taste for blood, are far more frightening.

Phantom in the photograph

In 1954, seven-year-old René Leret from near Lyon in France was given a kitten. He adored it, so his parents thought he would be devastated when a truck killed it a month later.

But René would not believe his pet was dead. He insisted that it was still with him, though nobody else could see it. He continued stroking it, feeding it and talking to it.

A well-known French ghost investigator visited René. He was amazed to see a photograph of René with his kitten, taken three weeks after the kitten's death...

Black dogs

Stories of phantom black dogs are told in several countries, but most come from Britain. In some of them, the dog has one blazing eye. In others, its paws point the wrong way. Sometimes, the phantom dog has no head, only a bleeding stump at its neck.

Usually, black dogs appear briefly, then simply vanish. Seeing one always spells bad luck, though, as the Vaughn family from Shropshire, England, discovered.

Dog of doom

For centuries, so this version of the story goes, a black dog had invariably appeared just before any member of the Vaughn family died. Mr. Vaughn knew about this tradition, but did not tell his wife in case it scared her.

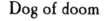

When one of their children fell ill, Mrs. Vaughn made one of her frequent trips to the sickroom. Almost immediately, she came shrieking back downstairs, begging her husband to get rid of the huge, black dog sitting on the child's bed. Appalled, Mr. Vaughn knew at once what the appearance of the mysterious animal meant.

He raced upstairs, knowing in his heart that it was hopeless, only to find his beloved child already dead and the grisly phantom black dog gone.

Runaway cattle

In the 1800s, cowboys used to drive huge herds of cattle across the North American plains. In Texas, one cowboy recklessly drove his herd right through a newly built ranch because it blocked his usual route. The cattle stampeded and trampled all the farm workers to death. The doomed ranch later became known as Stampede.

On moonlit nights, people say a ghostly herd of cattle still stampedes across the Texas sky.

Monster cat

In 1968, Margaret O'Brien bought a deserted old house at Killakee in Southern Ireland. One evening, she was horrified to see a black cat the size of a dog in her hallway, its red-flecked eyes flashing. Builders working in the house also saw the cat and heard a deep voice saying, 'You cannot see me. You don't even know who I am.'

Margaret finally asked a priest to rid her house of the monstrous cat. It was never seen again.

Werewolves

There are many stories of humans becoming animals, or werebeasts. Some can be transformed at any time, others only change at night or when there is a full moon. Werebeasts feel they must go in search of human prey before becoming a person again. Most stories concern werewolves.

France has the most werewolf stories. In one, a young boy named Jean Grenier told a court that he was a werewolf and had eaten fifty children. He enjoyed it very much, he said.

In 1589, in Germany, Peter Stump told a court that he had a magic belt that helped him turn into a werewolf. Nobody ever found his belt, but Peter was still tortured and burned to death.

In a Russian story, a woman's servant becomes a wolf while she is out walking. Her dogs chase the wolf, snapping at its eyes. She returns home to find her servant blinded.

Magic belt

UNITED STATES
Texas stampede

Navaho Indians in North America believed witches disguised themselves inside wolves' bodies.

Wolf-boy

Killakee

ENGLAND
IRELAND

Lyon **GERMANY**
FRANCE

Blinded servant

RUSSIA In Russia, tales of werebears are common.

In India, people are said to become weretigers.

AFRICA

SOUTH AMERICA
Werejaguars roam the South American rainforests.

INDIA

Stories of werecrocodiles are told in North Africa.

N
W E
S

Ghosts of North America

The United States and Canada seem positively packed with poltergeists, phantoms and ghostly gatherings. North American ghouls can be particularly nasty.

Story tellers

The first Americans, the Indian tribes, sat around their camp fires telling stories of spirits and ghosts. One sad story tells of the ghost of the last member of the Mohawk tribe paddling his canoe up the Mohawk River in the eastern USA. He is said to be looking for his people, killed by European settlers.

Indians also believed that ghosts appeared as 'dancing blue spirits', hovering above graves. Does this explain the mystery of the town of Silver Cliff, Colorado?

Ghostly lights

One night in the 1880s, some drunken silver-miners were lumbering home. As they swayed past the town's graveyard, they were shocked to see a soft blue light shimmering above each grave. They rushed to tell the townspeople what they had seen, but few believed them.

A few weeks later, the mysterious lights were seen again, by sober people. Now they were taken very seriously.

CANADA

Amherst

UNITED STATES OF AMERICA

President Abraham Lincoln dreamed he would be assassinated. He was proved right on April 14, 1865.

Mohawk River

Niagara Falls

Silver Cliff

Washington

Robertson County

Georgia

N
W   E
S

Ghost experts spent long nights in the graveyard, waiting to see the lights. As late as the 1960s, experts investigated the phenomenon and could not find an explanation. Local people say the lights are the ghosts of poor miners buried in the graveyard, still searching for silver.

Miraculous rescue

Mining is a dangerous job, but building bridges near one of the world's biggest waterfall is just as risky. In 1940, Patrick Thompson, an engineer, was working near Niagara Falls on the border between Canada and the United States. One night, he fell into the river near the Falls. Rescuers tried to find him, but in vain. The swirling waters carried him to his death. Two years later, Thompson's son Kenneth also slipped into the water near the Falls. Unable to swim, he flailed closer and closer to certain death.

Suddenly, Kenneth felt an invisible force wrap itself around him, and heard a voice he recognized guiding him gently to safety. The voice was his father's...

House of horror

A less soothing voice filled the Walsingham family home in Georgia in 1891. Each night, screams and eerie laughter made sure nobody slept. During the day, Mr. Walsingham noticed a ghostly set of footprints appearing next to his own as he walked. His daughter felt a man's hand resting on her shoulder, but saw nothing when she looked in the mirror.

One night, as the family sat down to dinner, blood dripped onto the table and awful groans echoed from the room above. The family moved out. Mr. Walsingham remembered throwing out some bones when he moved into the house. Could this have offended a ghost?

Disappearing act

There are several versions of this legend, but the basics are always the same. This version begins on a cold, rainy night, somewhere in America. As a man drives home, he spots a teenage girl hitchhiking beside the road. She is alone and soaking wet, so he takes pity on her and offers her a lift.

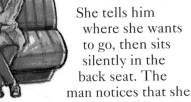

She tells him where she wants to go, then sits silently in the back seat. The man notices that she is shivering. He offers her his jacket, she takes it gratefully and falls asleep.

When the driver reaches the house the girl had asked to go to, she has vanished - and so has his jacket. Puzzled, he knocks on the door of the house and a tired-looking woman opens it. She is not surprised to hear his strange story, and tells him that the hitchhiker is her daughter, run down ten years earlier at the exact spot he had picked the girl up. She still seems to be trying to come home.

The man drives home, but he cannot forget the girl, or her story. The following day, he finds her grave in the local cemetery. Lying on top of it, neatly folded, is his jacket.

Dark threat

Several famous American spooky stories are about poltergeists, or 'noisy spirits'. They may be invisible, but the damage they do is all too real.

In 1817, 'something' began haunting the Bell family in Robertson County, Tennessee. They called it 'the Bell Witch'.

Whatever it was, it enjoyed pulling bedcovers off, slapping the family's faces and filling their house with shrieks and whistles. When Mr. Bell died suddenly in 1820, the Witch proudly said that she had poisoned him. His horrified family found a bottle of mysterious, smoky liquid; a tiny taste of it killed their cat. The Witch then vanished, promising to return in seven years. Apart from a few strange noises, she never has...so far.

Victim of terror

A poltergeist also made a family miserable in Amherst, Canada. The nineteen-year-old daughter of the Cox family, Esther, lived a life of torment for over a year.

The trouble began in 1889, when Esther and her sister heard strange noises coming from under their bed. Then, the house began to echo with deafening knocks, louder than the most violent thunderstorm. Worse, far worse, was still to come, though.

One night when the evil force was at work, poor Esther swelled up like a balloon and her hair stood on end. Next, threatening messages appeared on the walls of her bedroom and flaming matches dropped onto Esther's bed. Not surprisingly, she fell ill and left the house. When she returned, the mysterious happenings gradually stopped. Esther Cox became famous, but she has since been suspected of faking the events.

This photograph shows the Cox family house in Amherst, Nova Scotia, Canada.

13

Spirits of South America

South America seems to be a focus for amazing happenings and mysterious powers. Indian tribes believe that spirits roam in the dense rainforests, and unexplained forces are at play elsewhere, too...

Signs to spaceships?

On the Nazca plateau, in Peru, huge shapes of animals, birds and patterns were cut into the land over 1,500 years ago by American Indians. Some experts think they were to please the Indians' gods. Others say they are messages for spaceships.

Shamans

Shamans are tribal priests. In Brazil, shamans claim to talk to spirits, see the future and cure diseases. When they die, they are buried far from their tribes in graves ringed by thorns. Shamans say that their spirit then enters a jaguar and silently stalks the forest.

Spirit power

American Indians believe that everything in the forest has its own spirit. The Aztecs, who lived over 500 years ago, crammed their temples with golden offerings to their gods. When the Spanish conquered them in the 1500s, many of these temples were looted and destroyed. But legends spread about one temple which had escaped the looting and many people set out to find it. Nobody survived the attempt. Each one was found mysteriously crushed to death outside the temple walls.

Rhea's revenge

It seems that animal spirits are especially powerful in South America. If any of the Lengua tribe kills a rhea - a large bird rather like an ostrich - they fear its furious spirit will chase them back to their village and kill them. So they drop clumps of the rhea's feathers by the roadside all the way home. If the bird's spirit follows, it has to stop and check every clump, giving them time to get home safely.

Caribbean mystery

On the island of Haiti, people whisper about sorcerors bringing corpses back to 'life' as mindless zombies. The dead in a graveyard in Bridgetown, Barbados, were also disturbed in the early 1800s. On five occasions, when the Chase family opened their vault to lay another body to rest, the coffins inside had mysteriously moved.

Alien passenger

Since the 1950s, there have been numerous sightings of Unidentified Flying Objects, or U.F.O.s, over South America. In 1957, they say one took a farm-worker for a ride.

Could it have been the spirits of the temple protecting it from looters?

Antonio Villas Boas, a South American farm-worker, said that aliens pushed him on board a U.F.O.

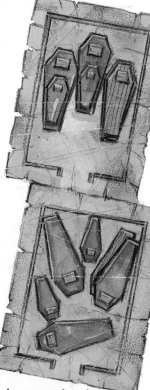

The coffins were placed as in the top picture on the right on July 17, 1819.

When the vault was opened on April 18, 1820, the coffins were rearranged as in the lower picture.

Somehow, the marble slab sealing the entrance to the vault had not been touched.
  Some of the coffins were made of lead, and tremendously heavy. It had taken eight men to lift them into the vault. There were also no footprints in the sand specially sprinkled on the floor. This case still puzzles ghost experts today.

Alien force

Experts were also unable to help a Brazilian family, plagued by a malicious poltergeist. On July 18, 1972, the Riberio family were sitting in their apartment in Sorocaba, Brazil. Without any warning, furniture began flying around the room. A brick hit Mr. Riberio's head. Imagine his small daughter's terror when 'something' grabbed a boiling kettle from her, badly scalding her arm.

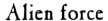

Brazilian ghost experts could not offer the desperate Riberios any advice. They went to stay with relatives, but the poltergeist followed, wrecking their home too. Eventually the Riberios left Sorocaba and were never heard of again.

The lady in black

Family tragedies are also at the heart of the next two well-known legends. In one, a Mexican widow is in love with a young man. Infatuated with him, she drowns her own children because he does not want them. As soon as she realizes the terrible thing she has done, she drowns herself as well. People say that her sad spirit, shrouded in black, still wanders beside rivers in Mexico, weeping for her children. Anyone seeing her is doomed to die within a year, in one version of the legend.

Gaucho

Millions of cattle graze on the grasslands of Argentina, called the pampas. Men called gauchos herd them up. One story tells of a gaucho who spent every free moment weaving. His finest items were ponchos - warm, woven capes with a slit at the neck for the head to go through. One day, he began work on a new poncho. He soon became obsessed with it, completely ignoring his family and his work, thinking only of what patterns he could weave into his poncho.

Fiesta

The gaucho heard of a big fiesta being held at a local ranch. He worked day and night to finish his poncho. The first half of it was superb, but the rest was poorly-woven. As he rode to the fiesta, a huge bird of prey swooped over the lonely gaucho. The horse reared in terror, throwing him to the ground.

Punishment

Claws dug into the gaucho's flesh, and fists thumped him. A stern voice said, 'You neglected your family and your work for that miserable poncho.' The voice then sentenced him to wander the pampas forever. He can still be seen today, some people say.

MEXICO
HAITI   CARIBBEAN
CENTRAL AMERICA
BARBADOS   Bridgetown
N
W   E
PERU
S
Nazca Plateau
BRAZIL
BOLIVIA
Sorocaba
In Bolivia, silver-miners leave gifts for a spirit called Pio, who rules over the mines, they say.
Pampas
ATLANTIC OCEAN
ARGENTINA
PACIFIC OCEAN

Ghostly messages

Ghosts often have a good reason to haunt people. Some have an urgent message or warning to deliver. Others seem to feel the need to visit loved ones just before they die, as if to say farewell.

The black velvet ribbon

A warning lies at the heart of this story, set in Ireland in the 1700s. Lord Tyrone and his sister, Lady Beresford, promised that when one of them died, he or she would visit the other for a final time...as a ghost.

One morning, Lady Beresford appeared with a black velvet ribbon around one wrist. She announced that she knew her brother had died the previous Tuesday, and that she was expecting a baby boy.

Lady Beresford was proved right. News came of Lord Tyrone's death and she bore a son seven months later. Lord Beresford never queried his wife's predictions, or the black velvet ribbon she always wore.

Years passed and Lord Beresford died. His wife married again, but was unhappy. One day, at a family party, she looked merrier than she had in years. She revealed that today was her forty-eighth birthday.

When an old friend said that official records showed she was only forty-seven, Lady Beresford rushed from the room crying, 'You have just signed my death warrant.' Her son followed her as she fled.

She confessed that Lord Tyrone's ghost had visited her years before, to reveal his death, her pregnancy and that she would die in her forty-seventh year. His spectral touch had shrivelled her wrist.

Before midnight on her birthday, Lady Beresford was dead. When her grieving son unwound the ribbon on her wrist, he found that it was indeed withered by the ghost's fingers, just as she had told him.

Dicing with death

People can be prepared for physical danger, perhaps even expect to encounter it, but they cannot predict supernatural forces. In 1975, an expedition set off to climb Mount Everest in the Himalayas, in Nepal. The team was skilled in mountaineering and expected perils ahead but nothing could prepare them for what they had to face.

Mystery message

The expedition leader, Chris Bonington, did not tell his team of a letter he had received before they left. The ghost of a mountaineer who had died on Everest in 1924 had warned the letter-writer that tragedy would strike Bonington's team. The exact details of what the ghost said would happen were written in another letter he had sealed and locked up in the Bank of England, in London.

Apparition

On the night of September 26, one of the climbers, Nick Estcourt, was walking from camp 4 to camp 5, higher up Everest. It was almost dawn but the moon only shed a watery light on the snowy slopes. Suddenly Estcourt felt he was being followed. He turned and saw another climber, black against the snow. As he looked again, it vanished.

Did Estcourt see the ghost forseen in the sealed letter?

Ghostly visitors

Mourners at the funeral of Father McSweeny in Ireland were shocked to see the man they had just buried walk past them as they left the chuchyard. Apparently, the ghost had also visited his terrified mother during his own funeral.

In the 18th century, a ghost visited the widow of the Dutch ambassador to Sweden, saying her husband had died owing him 25,000 Dutch guilders. Soon afterwards, her husband's ghost appeared and told her where to find proof that the debt was paid.

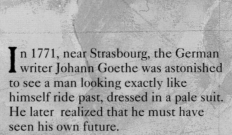

SWEDEN

Black ribbon

Dutch debt

White Lady

Dead priest

London

Berlin

FRANCE

IRELAND

Pale rider

Strasbourg

ATLANTIC OCEAN

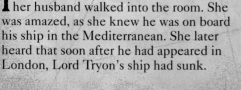

Soldier's goodbye

Death on Everest

NEPAL

Sinking ship

There are many stories of ghostly apparitions of men who died in the First World War. Captain Bowyer-Bower's spirit 'visited' his sister in India, his three-year-old niece and a family friend shortly before he died in battle in France.

INDIAN OCEAN

In 1893, Lady Tryon was in London when her husband walked into the room. She was amazed, as she knew he was on board his ship in the Mediterranean. She later heard that soon after he had appeared in London, Lord Tryon's ship had sunk.

In 1771, near Strasbourg, the German writer Johann Goethe was astonished to see a man looking exactly like himself ride past, dressed in a pale suit. He later realized that he must have seen his own future.

For over 300 years, a ghost called The White Lady warned of a death in the Prussian royal family. Even since their palace in Berlin was destroyed in 1945, people have seen a white figure floating silently over the site of the lost palace.

Tragedy

When he reached his destination, he telephoned the camp he had come from. He was told that nobody had followed him from the team and that no other climbers were in the area. Estcourt was puzzled, but did not tell anyone what he had seen until much later.

That afternoon, tragedy struck. A cameraman called Mick Burke died as he tried to reach the summit of Everest in a blizzard.

Back in London, Bonington felt drawn to open the sealed letter in the Bank of England. It said that a ghost would appear on Everest during the expedition, and that one of his climbers would die.

Vampires

Vampires are sometimes described as weird, bloodsucking animals, but most are said to be dead people that rise from their graves to drink blood. They look horribly alive in their coffins, even though they are dead. Anyone bitten by a vampire is supposed to become one too, and be very hard to kill. Some vampire stories are based on the bloodthirsty habits of real people.

Vlad the Impaler

Prince Vlad Dracula ruled Wallachia, now Romania, in the 1400s. He probably inspired Bram Stoker to write his famous book, *Count Dracula*.

Vlad got his ghastly nickname, 'the Impaler', from his habit of impaling people on wooden stakes. He also nailed people's hats to their heads and chopped people into pieces and made their families eat them. His home was Bran Castle. Tourists can now go on special *Dracula* tours in the region.

Bloodbaths

Countess Elizabeth of Bathory in Hungary liked bathing in the blood of young girls. She thought it kept her youthful-looking. When she had murdered 650 girls, horrified officials shut her up in one room of her castle to starve to death.

Arnold Paole

In 1729, Arnold Paole, a Serbian soldier, was attacked by a vampire in Greece. He ate earth from its grave and smeared himself with its blood to avoid becoming a vampire too.

Arnold returned to Hungary and worked on a farm. He died when a farm cart fell on top of him. The villagers buried him with great sadness, but grief soon turned to horror.

People saw Arnold haunting the village. Four villagers grew weak and died. Officials dug up Arnold's body to find him looking alive, with fresh blood around his mouth.

Over the next seventeen days, the villagers killed over twenty vampires that Arnold had bitten. They drove stakes through their hearts, chopped off their heads and burned their bodies.

Headless teacher

Liu was a teacher in China. When his wife went to wake him up one morning, she found his head had been chopped off.

Horrified, she ran for help, but was soon put into jail for murdering her husband. Investigations found no other suspect.

Months later, some villagers passed a coffin with an open lid. They looked inside, and saw a hideous, hairy vampire clutching poor Liu's head. The vampire was burned, and the innocent widow set free.

Vampires around the world

In Malaysia, vampires are shaped like flying heads. They suck blood from victims with their noses.

Japanese vampires are very cunning. They can take on any shape, even that of their dead victim.

In Portugal, a bird-like vampire is especially feared. Stories said she used to drink children's blood.

Mara vampire

DENMARK
GERMANY
ROMANIA

Nachzehrer

HUNGARY

Bloodbaths

PrinceVlad

CHINA

Cunning vampires

GREECE

PORTUGAL

Bird vampire

Arnold Paole

Headless teacher

JAPAN

Flying head

ATLANTIC OCEAN

PACIFIC OCEAN

INDIAN OCEAN

MALAYSIA

Langsuir

N
W   E
S

The Mara vampire in Denmark is said to suck the blood of sleeping young men. Only knives scare her off.

Malaysian vampires, or langsuirs, drink blood through a hole in the back of their neck. According to tradition, they look like birds.

German vampires, or nachzehrer, chew their clothes while clutching one of their thumbs. Some of them even resemble pigs.

Haunted Europe

By day, the towns and cities of Europe bustle with activity, their palaces, castles and cathedrals packed with tourists. But at night, when the sights are deserted and dark, it's easy to imagine the ghosts of people who once lived there walking the streets once more.

Athens in Greece is one of Europe's oldest cities. It is also the setting for a ghost story 2,000 years old. A writer called Pliny the Younger told it in a letter to a friend in Rome.

Several French castles are said to be haunted. Three you can visit are marked here.

One castle in the German Harz mountains is said to have a haunted bed.

In the Spanish city of Saragossa, a ghost once appeared that talked to people down a chimney.

HOLLAND
The Hague
Eisenach
Paris GERMANY
FRANCE Versailles
Blois
Chenonceaux
Azaye le Rideau
Turin
Saragossa
ITALY
GREECE
Athens

Chains and groans

It was not easy to find a house to rent in Athens, yet nobody wanted to rent one large house in a quiet part of the city. Many tenants had moved in, but none had managed to spend a whole night there. They had all fled in terror, saying they had seen the pale, wailing ghost of an old man, with heavy chains around his legs and wrists. His beard matted and filthy, he had shaken his chains at them in a pitiful attempt to be free, the scared tenants said. The vision was so horrible that one tenant had even died of shock.

A philosopher called Athenodorus moved into the empty house. Whether he was brave, or just foolish, nobody could decide...

A night visitor

One night, Athenodorus sat puzzling over a philosophical problem. He tried to concentrate, but the house was filled with the unmistakeable sound of metal chains dragging along the floor. As the noise grew louder, Athenodorus could ignore it no longer. He looked up to see exactly what every tenant before him had spoken of with such horror...the white-haired ghost of an old man, groaning pitifully and shaking his chains. The phantom silently beckoned Athenodorus to follow him. The lonely figure led him to an overgrown corner of the garden, pointed to the ground, then vanished.

The next day, Athenodorus told the local magistrate what had happened, and digging began in the garden. A twisted skeleton was found in the exact spot the ghost had pointed to, its limbs bound by rusty chains. The bones were dug up and properly buried, and the old man's ghost was never seen again.

Strange missile

Written in a castle in Germany, one man's diary tells of a far more menacing night visitor. The churchman Martin Luther protested against the Pope's wealth and pressed for reform during the 1500s. He made many enemies, so he hid in Wartburg Castle near Eisenach, in southern Germany.

One night, as Luther worked, he became aware of someone else in his tiny room. On the wall towered the horned shadow of a figure he recognized only too well, the Devil himself. Unafraid, Luther threw his pot of ink at him. The shadow vanished, but you can still see the ink-stain on the wall today.

Mischief or malice?

Business was brisk in a bar in Turin, Italy, in 1900. Then the strange noises began. Every night, the sound of smashing wine bottles in the cellar scared off most customers.

A ghost expert visited the bar and saw bottles shatter without being touched, furniture flying around and the landlord's clothes and shoes disappearing. The expert concluded that a poltergeist was using the energy, or 'power', that young people possess as they are growing up, to create chaos in the bar. Only if the person unwittingly providing the energy was removed would the problems cease.

The expert told the landlord to get rid of a teenage waiter. When he did, the mysterious happenings stopped.

Deathly drink

Not wine, but water, was the chosen weapon of a ghost in number 12, Westeinde Street, an old house in The Hague, Holland.

In the 1500s, a young woman called Catherine de Chasseur was married to the owner of the house. Living a life of luxury, she ran out of cash, so she started making counterfeit money. She was caught on February 11, 1541 and was gruesomely sentenced to be filled up with water until she died.

The original number 12, Westeinde, was pulled down in 1754 and rebuilt, but everyone who has lived there since poor Catherine's death felt that they were sharing the house with a ghost. Blankets were pulled off beds, doors opened and shut. Water was scattered around and taps left running, too. Some say they have seen a pale figure floating through the house, but the mischievous ghost of number 12, Westeinde usually prefers to act unseen.

A step back in time

One of the most intriguing French ghost stories is set in Versailles, a French town about 20 km (9 miles) from Paris. The town is famous for the huge, luxurious palace that the French King, Louis XIV, built there during the 1700s. The royal family visited it right up until they were executed in 1793, during the bloody French Revolution. Queen Marie Antoinette particularly loved a smaller palace inside the gardens of Versailles, called the Petit Trianon.

The Petit Trianon is a popular tourist attraction today.

© R.M.N. / Arnaudet

Strange messengers

Two English women were heading for the Petit Trianon in 1901. There were several paths ahead, and they were unsure which to take. When they saw two men dressed in long coats and three-cornered hats, the ladies thought them odd, but asked them for directions anyway. Suddenly, they felt the atmosphere change... things seemed so still and quiet, it felt unreal, they said later.

Feeling very uncomfortable, the ladies passed another man in a cloak and a large hat with a scarred, ugly face.

They walked hesitantly on until they reached the back of the Petit Trianon. Sitting on the lawn was a woman, wearing a white hat, cape and an old-fashioned dress. She looked at the

This plan shows the route the ladies took.

tourists, then turned away. The puzzled women were then led away by a man.

Marie Antoinette

Ghostly queen?

For the rest of their lives, the ladies were convinced that they had been back in time and seen Queen Marie Antoinette shortly before she was executed. They recognized her from portraits, they said. Nobody has ever completely succeeded in disproving their story.

Scarred man seen here.

Mysterious lady sat here, sketching.

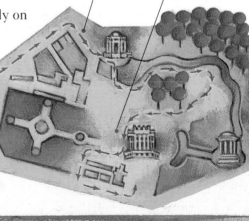

Haunted seas

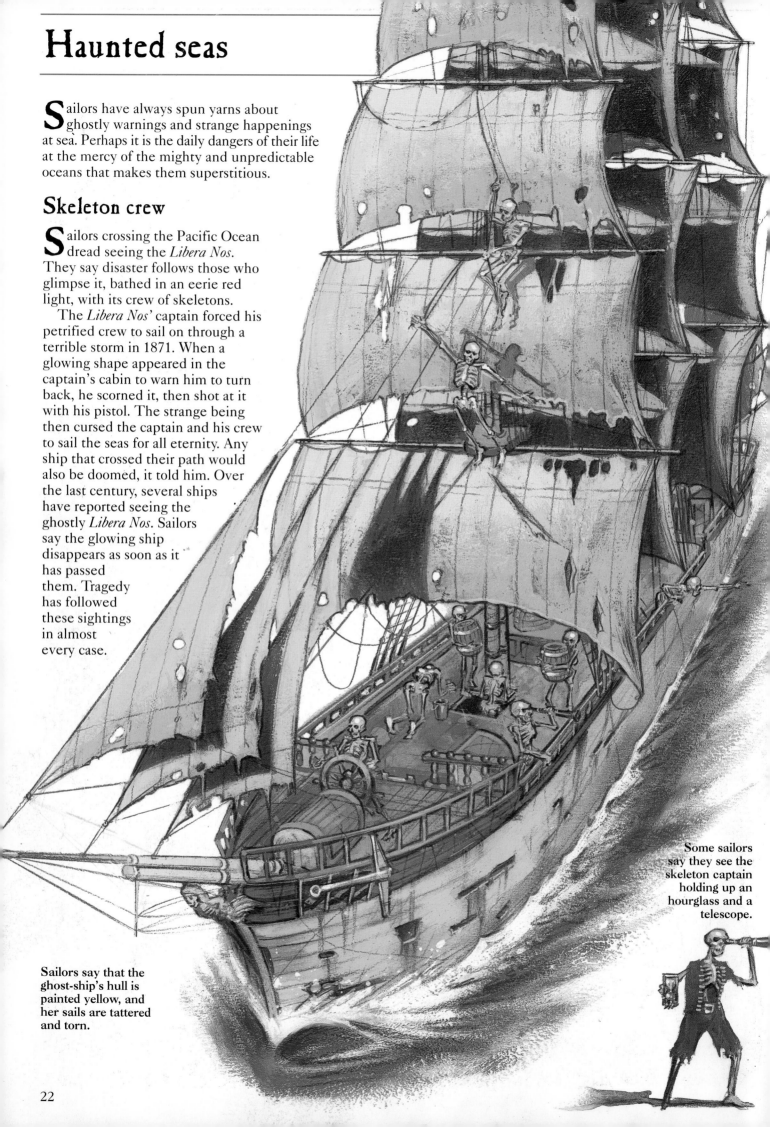

Sailors have always spun yarns about ghostly warnings and strange happenings at sea. Perhaps it is the daily dangers of their life at the mercy of the mighty and unpredictable oceans that makes them superstitious.

Skeleton crew

Sailors crossing the Pacific Ocean dread seeing the *Libera Nos*. They say disaster follows those who glimpse it, bathed in an eerie red light, with its crew of skeletons.

The *Libera Nos'* captain forced his petrified crew to sail on through a terrible storm in 1871. When a glowing shape appeared in the captain's cabin to warn him to turn back, he scorned it, then shot at it with his pistol. The strange being then cursed the captain and his crew to sail the seas for all eternity. Any ship that crossed their path would also be doomed, it told him. Over the last century, several ships have reported seeing the ghostly *Libera Nos*. Sailors say the glowing ship disappears as soon as it has passed them. Tragedy has followed these sightings in almost every case.

Sailors say that the ghost-ship's hull is painted yellow, and her sails are tattered and torn.

Some sailors say they see the skeleton captain holding up an hourglass and a telescope.

Spooky orders

In 1902, a sailing ship called the *Firebird* caught fire at sea. The seventy-four survivors leaped into four lifeboats, and were drifting on the open ocean. Meanwhile, a trading ship called the *James Gilbert* was heading for Bombay. As the helmsman, alone in the wheelhouse, steered north-east, he suddenly altered course so that the *James Gilbert* was able to rescue the survivors. The events leading to this rescue are most mysterious.

A man in captain's uniform came into the *James Gilbert's* wheelhouse. His face was horribly scarred. He ordered the helmsman to head nor' nor' east, which he did.

The new course took the *James Gilbert* straight to the drifting survivors of the *Firebird*. A falling mast had killed their unfortunate captain, they said.

Later, a man's body, in captain's uniform, was spotted. The helmsman recognized the scarred face and realized he had taken orders from a ghost.

Scary sea stories

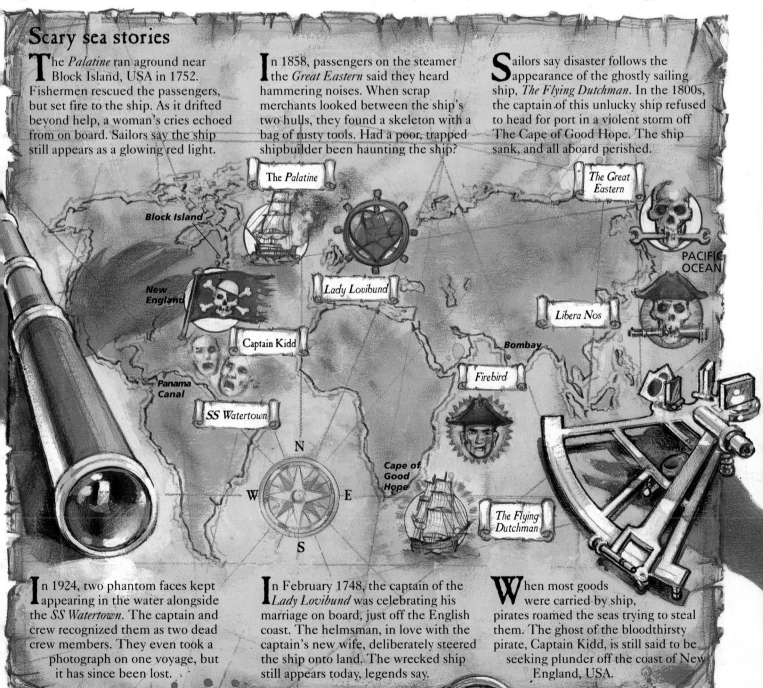

The *Palatine* ran aground near Block Island, USA in 1752. Fishermen rescued the passengers, but set fire to the ship. As it drifted beyond help, a woman's cries echoed from on board. Sailors say the ship still appears as a glowing red light.

In 1858, passengers on the steamer the *Great Eastern* said they heard hammering noises. When scrap merchants looked between the ship's two hulls, they found a skeleton with a bag of rusty tools. Had a poor, trapped shipbuilder been haunting the ship?

Sailors say disaster follows the appearance of the ghostly sailing ship, *The Flying Dutchman*. In the 1800s, the captain of this unlucky ship refused to head for port in a violent storm off The Cape of Good Hope. The ship sank, and all aboard perished.

The *Palatine*

Block Island

New England

Captain Kidd

Panama Canal

SS Watertown

Lady Lovibund

The Great Eastern

PACIFIC OCEAN

Libera Nos

Bombay

Firebird

Cape of Good Hope

The Flying Dutchman

N
W · E
S

In 1924, two phantom faces kept appearing in the water alongside the *SS Watertown*. The captain and crew recognized them as two dead crew members. They even took a photograph on one voyage, but it has since been lost.

In February 1748, the captain of the *Lady Lovibund* was celebrating his marriage on board, just off the English coast. The helmsman, in love with the captain's new wife, deliberately steered the ship onto land. The wrecked ship still appears today, legends say.

When most goods were carried by ship, pirates roamed the seas trying to steal them. The ghost of the bloodthirsty pirate, Captain Kidd, is still said to be seeking plunder off the coast of New England, USA.

More sea ghosts

Sailors tell many a chilling tale. It may be just their imagination at work, or perhaps sailors have seen things out on the vast, silent oceans that you and I cannot begin to imagine.

The *Octavius*

The dreadful fate of the crew of the *Octavius* was never a mystery, but what followed was a nautical miracle.

In 1775, the whaling ship *Herald* came across the battered *Octavius* off the coast of Greenland. When nine sailors went below decks, they found the crew lying on their bunks wrapped in thick blankets, frozen to death. The dead captain was hunched over the ship's log. A pile of wood shavings showed that the crew's last desperate efforts to light a fire had been in vain.

Incredible voyage

The sailors from the *Herald* took the captain's log to prove what they had found, but left the *Octavius* to drift on the icy waters

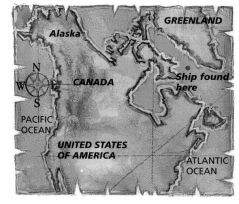

with its ghoulish cargo. When the *Herald*'s Captain Warren read the log his men had retrieved, he was astounded to read that the sea had first frozen around the *Octavius* north of Alaska in November 1762. Yet thirteen years later, he had found the ship thousands of miles east of Alaska. Captain Warren realized that the *Octavius* was the first ship to prove that there must be a north-west passage between the Atlantic and the Pacific Oceans.

The sailor was also frustrated to realize that nobody would ever know the exact route the tragic ship had taken.

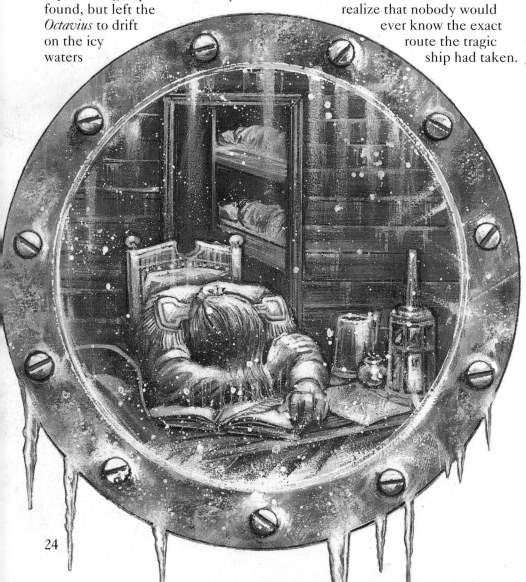

The *Mary Celeste*

One very famous sea tale began on November 4, 1872, when the brigantine Mary Celeste sailed out of New York bound for Genoa, Italy. Captain Benjamin Briggs, his wife Sarah, his daughter Sophia, and eight crew were on board.

On November 24, Briggs wrote in the ship's log that it was stormy. Next morning, he logged the ship's exact position...that was the last entry.

Ten days later, another brigantine, the *Dei Gratia*, saw the *Mary Celeste* drifting with nobody to be seen on board. Three sailors rowed across to her, but found no sign of anyone.

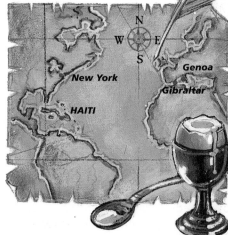

At the deserted breakfast table, it seemed that Captain Briggs had cut off the top of his boiled egg, but not yet eaten a spoonful. His wife's music was open on her melodeon, as if she had been playing it moments before. It seemed that the ship had been abandoned in great haste, but there was no clue as to why, or where the crew had gone. Captain Morehouse of the *Dei Gratia* was puzzled at how the deserted ship had stayed on course for ten days without a crew. He towed the abandoned ship into port at Gibraltar.

A public enquiry could not prove what had happened on board the *Mary Celeste*. Although the ship was sold, sailors said she was cursed and refused to sail on her. She finally sank off the island of Haiti in 1884, taking the secret of what really happened to Captain Briggs, his family and crew with her.

Eilean Mór

This is the tale of three lighthouse keepers on the Eilean Mór lighthouse on the Flannan Islands, off the rugged west coast of Scotland. On the night of December 15, 1900, two sailors on board the *Fairwind* swore they saw a boat packed with ghosts pass by, heading for the lighthouse. Later that night, the lamp of Eilean Mór lighthouse went out.

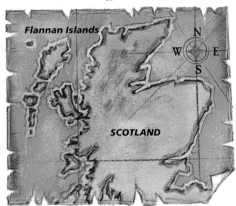

Flannan Islands

SCOTLAND

Vanished

Storms raged and ships were in danger of smashing against the rocks without the lighthouse to warn them. The *Hesperus* set out to discover what could be wrong. The sailors who went ashore found everything in order, but no sign of the three keepers - the only clue was that their waterproof clothes and boots were gone.

Tears and prayers

The sailors brought the lighthouse log back to their ship. What they read sent shivers down their spines. The head lighthouse keeper, Thomas Marshall, had written that he and his colleagues had spent their last days weeping and praying for protection from an unknown evil. Had they been affected by their lonely jobs, or had something unspeakably horrible happened?

Lights out

The three lighthouse keepers were never found. Locals believed they had joined the many ghosts who haunted the remote islands. They said that the boat full of ghosts seen by the *Fairwind*'s sailors had been on its way to collect the three men. Once they had joined the grisly crew, the lighthouse lamp had gone out.

The Bermuda Triangle

In 1918, a ship called the *Cyclops* vanished without trace in an area of open ocean near Bermuda, now known as The Bermuda Triangle. When five bomber aircraft disappeared there, too, in 1945, along with the plane sent to find them, a legend began.

Is it an alien force that makes the craft vanish, or the souls of slaves who died at sea, luring others to join them? Scientists say that extra-strong electromagnetism makes compasses go wrong in this area. Whatever the cause, The Bermuda Triangle remains a place most people prefer not to visit.

UNITED STATES OF AMERICA

ATLANTIC OCEAN

The Bermuda Triangle

The Bahamas

N E W S

CUBA

HAITI

Over 1,000 people and 120 vehicles have disappeared without known cause in The Bermuda Triangle.

China and Japan

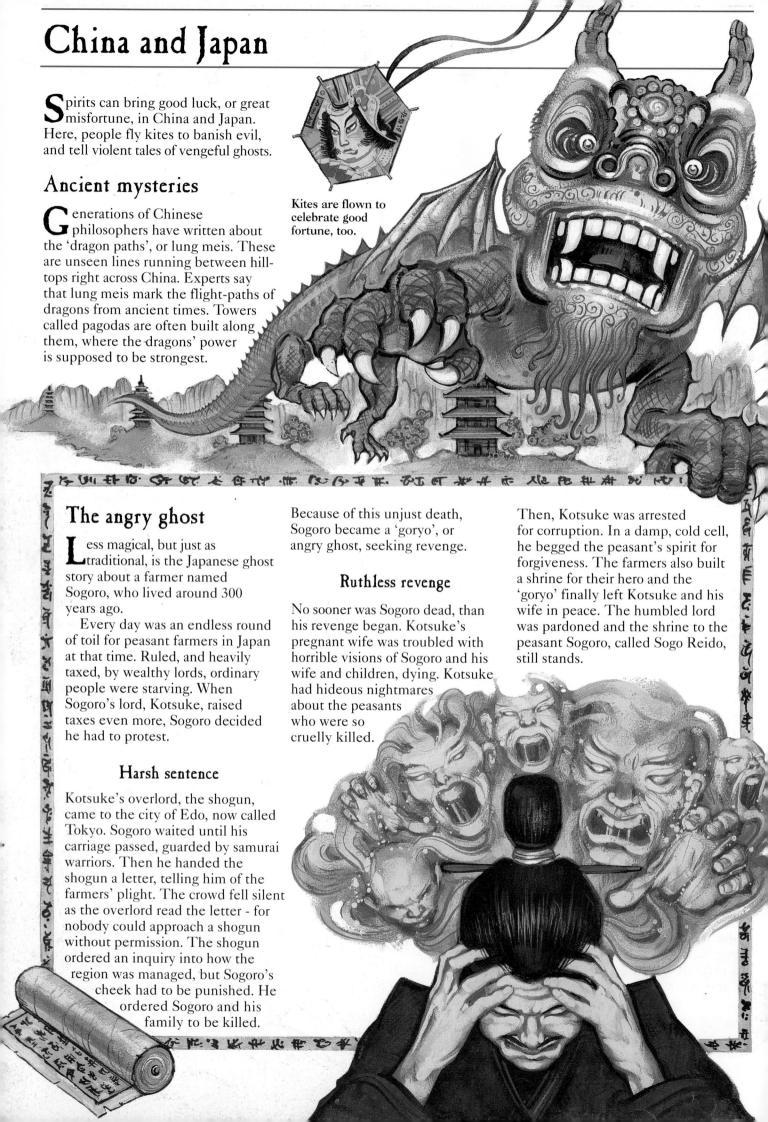

Spirits can bring good luck, or great misfortune, in China and Japan. Here, people fly kites to banish evil, and tell violent tales of vengeful ghosts.

Ancient mysteries

Generations of Chinese philosophers have written about the 'dragon paths', or lung meis. These are unseen lines running between hill-tops right across China. Experts say that lung meis mark the flight-paths of dragons from ancient times. Towers called pagodas are often built along them, where the dragons' power is supposed to be strongest.

Kites are flown to celebrate good fortune, too.

The angry ghost

Less magical, but just as traditional, is the Japanese ghost story about a farmer named Sogoro, who lived around 300 years ago.

Every day was an endless round of toil for peasant farmers in Japan at that time. Ruled, and heavily taxed, by wealthy lords, ordinary people were starving. When Sogoro's lord, Kotsuke, raised taxes even more, Sogoro decided he had to protest.

Harsh sentence

Kotsuke's overlord, the shogun, came to the city of Edo, now called Tokyo. Sogoro waited until his carriage passed, guarded by samurai warriors. Then he handed the shogun a letter, telling him of the farmers' plight. The crowd fell silent as the overlord read the letter - for nobody could approach a shogun without permission. The shogun ordered an inquiry into how the region was managed, but Sogoro's cheek had to be punished. He ordered Sogoro and his family to be killed.

Because of this unjust death, Sogoro became a 'goryo', or angry ghost, seeking revenge.

Ruthless revenge

No sooner was Sogoro dead, than his revenge began. Kotsuke's pregnant wife was troubled with horrible visions of Sogoro and his wife and children, dying. Kotsuke had hideous nightmares about the peasants who were so cruelly killed.

Then, Kotsuke was arrested for corruption. In a damp, cold cell, he begged the peasant's spirit for forgiveness. The farmers also built a shrine for their hero and the 'goryo' finally left Kotsuke and his wife in peace. The humbled lord was pardoned and the shrine to the peasant Sogoro, called Sogo Reido, still stands.

Love conquers death

This Chinese story is about a husband and wife who loved each other dearly. When the wife died, the husband visited a well where ghosts gathered, broke a coin in half and threw one half into the deep well.

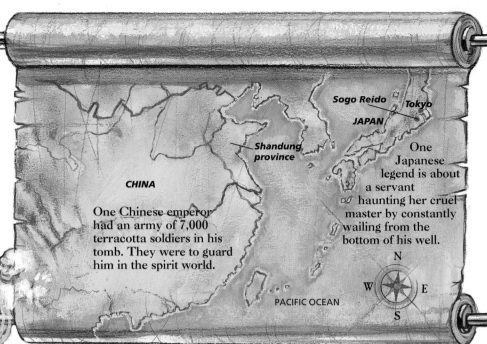

Sogo Reido Tokyo
JAPAN

Shandung province

CHINA

One Chinese emperor had an army of 7,000 terracotta soldiers in his tomb. They were to guard him in the spirit world.

One Japanese legend is about a servant haunting her cruel master by constantly wailing from the bottom of his well.

N
W   E
S

PACIFIC OCEAN

He had heard that this would help him talk to his dead wife. When her ghostly voice rose from the well, she sounded so sad that he persuaded her spirit to run away with him.

When they reached a lonely house, the wife's ghost went inside to ask for a drink. She did not return, so the husband went into the house searching for her. He found no sign, but suddenly heard the cry of a newborn baby. The farmer's wife had just had a baby daughter. Strangely, the baby's right hand would not open.

The grief-stricken husband stayed at the farm as a servant, hoping that his wife's ghost would somehow return. Years slowly passed, and the baby girl became a woman. Still, she did not open her right hand.

Reunited

On her eighteenth birthday, the husband's patience was rewarded; the young woman slowly opened her right hand for the first time. Clasped inside it was the half coin he had thrown into the well so many years before. Reunited, the couple married again.

Ch'iang Schich

Many Chinese ghost stories are less romantic. Sometimes the dead walk again as monstrous corpses. If one of these, called a Ch'iang Shich, breathes on you, death is certain. This horrid tale begins one night at an inn in Shandung province, when four men stop to ask for a room for the night.

Hidden horror

The inn was full, but the landlord showed them to a lonely house on the edge of the town. There were five beds, but the landlord did not tell the men that his dead daughter-in-law lay concealed in one of them.

Three of the men fell asleep, but the fourth was restless. He was just slipping into a doze when a creaking noise jolted him from his comfortable state. Who, or what, was parting the curtain on the far side of the room?

The corpse awakes

He watched the pale corpse of a young woman move jerkily towards each of the three sleepers. The creature breathed three times over each man, killing him instantly. As the monster leaned over the fourth, the man held his breath, saving his life. Then he ran in terror.

The chase

The Ch'iang Schich pursued him, its claws outstretched to rip him to shreds. He found himself trapped against a tree as the creature leaped at him. The poor man fainted and slid helplessly down the tree trunk. When he came to, it was dawn. Above him was the lifeless monster, its claws embedded in the tree. He was safe, but never the same again.

Battle ghosts

Over the centuries, millions of people have died in warfare. Battlefields are places of noise, terror and death, so perhaps it's not surprising that the ghosts of those who die there return to haunt them. Some ghost hunters believe that battles can be somehow recorded in time, as if they had been filmed. These recordings sometimes replay themselves at the battle-site.

Replayed raid

A thousand years ago, Vikings in longboats sailed the seas, coming ashore only to rob and wreck. Witnesses have seen a rerun of a Viking raid on the Abbey of Iona, Scotland, which took place in the 10th century. They can even describe the abbey burning and what the Vikings stole.

Ghostly battles

The Greek army defeated the Persian army over 2,000 years ago, at the Battle of Marathon. Ever since that day in 490BC, many people say they have seen this great battle being replayed. They say they hear men fighting and horses neighing.

Between 1861 and 1865, the northern and southern states of the United States were at war. At the battle of Shiloh in 1862, 20,000 men died. Some say a nearby river ran red with blood. There have been ghostly replays of this horrific clash ever since.

In 1815, the French emperor Napoleon Bonaparte was defeated at Waterloo, Belgium. A few weeks later, people in a nearby town say that they saw phantom cavalry soldiers in the sky, and heard the dull boom of ghostly cannons.

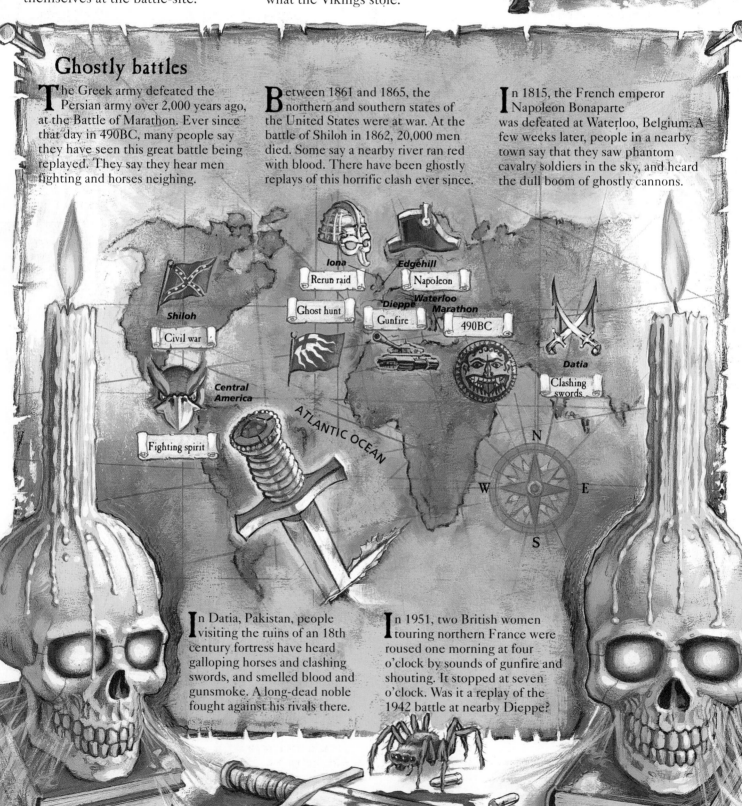

In Datia, Pakistan, people visiting the ruins of an 18th century fortress have heard galloping horses and clashing swords, and smelled blood and gunsmoke. A long-dead noble fought against his rivals there.

In 1951, two British women touring northern France were roused one morning at four o'clock by sounds of gunfire and shouting. It stopped at seven o'clock. Was it a replay of the 1942 battle at nearby Dieppe?

Fighting spirit

Aztec Indians in Central America believed that the spirits of birds and animals fought alongside their warriors in battles centuries ago. These legendary spirits were called Naguals. The greater the warrior, the more powerful the Nagual. If the warrior or the Nagual was killed, the other died, too.

In the 1500s, Spanish armies went to conquer the Aztecs. At one battle, an Aztec chief was guarded by a Nagual in the shape of a huge bird. A Spanish general, Pedro de Alvarado, killed the Nagual, and was amazed to see the chief fall dead too, without a wound on him.

Spanish soldiers, like Pedro de Alvarado, were called conquistadores, meaning conquerors.

A chief could become the shape of his Nagual, to hide from enemies.

Spooks in the sky

A famous investigation into a replayed ghost battle took place in England over 300 years ago. A violent clash took place at Edgehill in October 1642, during the English Civil War. One side, the Cavaliers, supported the king, Charles I. The other, the Roundheads, supported his opponent, a politician named Oliver Cromwell. Here's what is supposed to have happened on this early ghost hunt.

A few weeks after the battle, people near Edgehill spoke of seeing it being fought again, in the sky this time, by ghostly soldiers.

Charles I sent a team of trusted friends to Edgehill. They saw the phantom battle, too, and even recognized a famous Cavalier prince.

For centuries the battle was replayed on its anniversary in October, and at Christmas. Recently the recording seems faded, rather like a worn-out tape.

The mysterious East

In the bustling cities of India and on the windswept mountains of Tibet, the supernatural is a part of life. Ghosts like those in the West are rare, but there are many other marvels.

Life after death

Many people in India and Tibet believe that when someone dies, they are born again in another body, or reincarnated. In Tibet, the head of the Buddhist faith is the Dalai Lama. When he dies, Tibetan Buddhists believe that his spirit is born again as the spirit of a young boy. The boy must prove that he knows about his previous lives to be accepted as genuine. The present Dalai Lama's spirit even remembered where his predecessor had kept his false teeth.

Unwelcome guest

People in Tibet also believe that the spirits can be brought to 'life' by intense meditation. These spirits are called 'tulpas'. In the early 1900s, a French journalist called Alexandra David-Neel learned to meditate and created the tulpa of a fat monk. He was good company for a while, but soon became a nuisance. It took her six months to 'think him away' again.

Murdered

In the 1950s, a Canadian doctor called Ian Stevenson began researching reincarnation in the East. He interviewed many children who said they remembered previous lives. One Indian boy called Ravi Shankar remembered that he had once been a boy called Munna. He said he had been murdered by a barber and a washerwoman, who had cut his throat with a long, jagged knife.

Stevenson discovered that a boy called Munna had indeed been murdered in this brutal way six months before Ravi's birth. The suspects were a barber and a washerwoman. Although Dr. Stevenson could never prove that Munna had been reincarnated, Ravi did have a long, wide scar on his neck which nobody could explain.

Powers of the mind

In India, men called fakirs train their minds with an intensive form of meditation and exercise called yoga. They can lie on beds of nails or walk over burning coals without feeling pain. Some can even defy death.

Apparently, Subbayar Pullavar levitated for four minutes in 1936.

Buried alive

In 1835, a famous fakir called Haridas survived being buried alive for four months. He prepared his body by eating only milk and yogurt, closed his ears with wax to keep insects out, and crossed his legs. His breathing slowed down and doctors could hardly feel his pulse. To add to the test, Haridas was buried in a padlocked coffin and barley seeds were strewn on top. Forty days later, the barley was growing and the padlocks were still locked. Inside the coffin, the fakir was exactly as he had been buried. An hour later, he just walked away.

CHINA

TIBET
NEPAL

INDIA

N

W   E

S

The ape-like yet-teh, or abominable snowman, is said to roam the mountains of Nepal.

West meets East

India was governed by Britain for many years up until 1947. There are several vivid stories of Westerners encountering forces they did not understand in India, of which these two are sobering examples.

The first tale begins in the 1870s, as an English General, Henry Beresford of the Indian Army, and his wife, were riding along in their carriage.

Suddenly, Mrs. Beresford gripped her husband's arm and shrieked, 'Stop, Henry, can't you see her?' Her husband, startled and annoyed, tried to stop the carriage quickly.

Mrs. Beresford said she had seen an Indian servant woman, or ayah, in the road and they had run her over. The General looked, but there was nobody to be seen.

From that moment, his wife had no peace. She saw the ayah everywhere. Her husband feared she was ill and summoned their daughter, Barbara, from England.

Barbara could not see the ghost, but she took her mother to an Indian doctor who at once recognized the persecutor as a kind of witch called a kattidya.

He said that only if she dared tell the witch to go away would it leave. One night, Barbara was startled awake in the room she shared with her mother - and saw the ayah, grinning wildly.

The witch's hands were gripping her mother's neck and squeezing tightly. Barbara screamed. The ayah turned to her, relaxing her grip for a few crucial seconds..

Mrs. Beresford managed to murmer, 'Be gone, haunt me no more' and was tossed into the air and flung to the ground, before the ayah vanished - for good.

Terror of the tiger

Charles de Silva was hunting in the Indian jungle in the 1880s. As he stalked a tiger one night, a pitiful blind leper appeared before him, his skin horribly whitened by the disease. At that moment, a tiger's roar echoed out. The Englishman fled, but heard the leper's screams as the tiger pounced.

Man-eater

De Silva could not forget the leper, or the tiger. His Indian servants warned him that the leper had been a powerful sorceror and would return to haunt the man who had left him to die. When de Silva heard of a man-eating tiger, white with leprosy, he knew that the dead leper's spirit had found a new home.

Doggedly, he pursued and managed to shoot the tiger as it devoured its latest victim.

Avenged

However, before long the tiger reappeared, poised to leap at de Silva's wife, son and servant. De Silva fired, the leper's ghost rose before him, then tiger and leper disappeared. The servant lay dead and his son's face was cruelly scored by the tiger's claws. Within a week, the boy died of leprosy.

The leper, in the form of a tiger, took his terrible revenge.

Pyramids and pharaohs

The Pyramids have towered over the desert at Giza in Egypt for over 3,000 years. How the Ancient Egyptians built them is one of the world's great marvels. Why they did, is one of its most intriguing secrets.

Pyramid power

During the 1800s, archeologists flocked to Egypt to excavate the Pyramids. Some experts theorized that they were stairways leading to Heaven. Others, that they were arranged to align with major stars. Some mathematicians thought that a line drawn from the Great Pyramid of King Cheops divided the world exactly in half, and that the Pyramids marked the middle of the world.

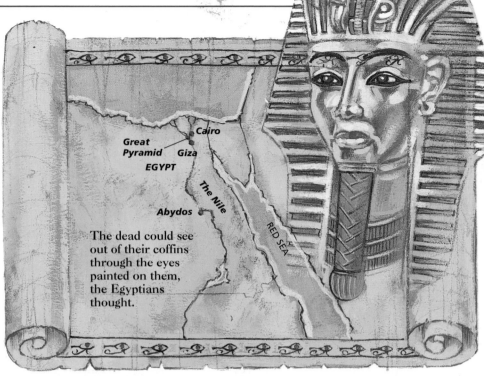

The dead could see out of their coffins through the eyes painted on them, the Egyptians thought.

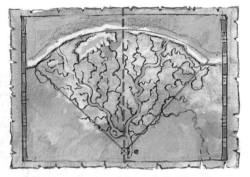

Old map of pyramids and dividing line.

Stopping the rot

One of the most unusual theories about the purpose of the Pyramids looked at how their shape seemed to have the power to stop things rotting. Experts from around the world built small pyramids and found that if they put meat or fruit inside them, it did not rot. A Frenchman called Antoine Bovis even put a dead cat inside a model pyramid: it did not decompose, but just dried out.

Razor sharp

The pyramid shape has another strange power, too. Blunt razor blades placed inside a model pyramid become sharp again. It only works, though, if the blade faces in the same direction as the main chamber inside King Cheops' pyramid. Nobody has managed to explain why.

Disturbed

Whether the Ancient Egyptians realized the powers their Pyramids seem to possess, we do not know. They built the Pyramids to last forever, though, and sealed them carefully so that their pharaohs' bodies would not be disturbed as they journeyed to another life after death.

The Egyptians left gifts and food for the dead to use in the next life.

Tutankhamun's tomb

In November 1922, the British archeologist Howard Carter opened the tomb of the Pharaoh Tutankhamun, who died more than 1350 years before Christ was born.
  Some say that Carter quickly hid a stone tablet at the entrance to the tomb. It bore the message, 'Death will slay with his wings whoever disturbs the Pharaoh's peace' in Egyptian symbols called hieroglyphics. Perhaps he should have heeded this clear and direful warning.

Poisoned

Over the next four years, twenty-two people connected with the opening of Tutankhamun's tomb died strange deaths. Many of them just seemed to lose the will to live. Some experts thought that the Egyptians may have sealed a poison in their tombs that still had the power to kill thousands of years later. Others thought that the deadly germs of ancient diseases could have been left in the tomb by the bearers of the pharaoh's coffin, and been 'caught' by whoever entered the tomb and breathed them in. Carter's financial backer, Lord Carnarvon, later received evidence of the powers the Ancient Egyptians possessed in a letter from a close friend, Count Louis Hamon.

Hand of doom

Hamon worked as a kind of healer. He had been given an unusual gift by a grateful patient in Egypt - the mummified hand of a princess who had died in Tutankhamun's time. Her father, pharaoh Akhenaten, had cut off her hand after an argument. Without it, she could not enter the afterlife. Her hand was buried near the Pyramids.

Hamon and his wife locked the shrivelled hand in a safe for over thirty years. In October 1922, they opened it, and were horrified to see that the hand was plump and fresh. The princess's flesh seemed to be returning to life....

Shocking sight

Countess Hamon insisted that the hand should be destroyed. Her husband placed it in the fireplace and read some of the 'Book of the Dead', a book of funeral prayers and spells written by the Ancient Egyptians. As his incantation came to a close, the figure of a young woman, dressed in the glittering clothes of the pharaoh's family, shimmered in the air before the petrified couple. One of her arms had no hand.

The figure then vanished, as did the hand in the fireplace. Count Hamon and his wife cowered in shock, unable to move.

Too late

Four days later, recovering in hospital, Hamon read that Carter and his friend Lord Carnarvon were about to enter Tutankhamun's tomb. He wrote, warning his friend to take care, but his letter did not arrive in time to stop them. Carnarvon and his wife were among the twenty-two people who died from what was later called 'The curse of the Pharaohs'.

Dorothy Eady

For one young English girl, the pharaohs' curse was also very real. From 1907, when she was three years old, Dorothy Eady began to say that she had lived in the time of Pharaoh Sety I, almost 3,500 years ago. She said that she had been Sety's mistress, Bentreshyt, who had been forced to kill herself once the affair was known.

Mummified head of Pharaoh Sety I

Strange knowledge

Dorothy studied hieroglyphics and went to live in Egypt. She seemed to know about everyday life in Ancient Egypt and could walk around ancient temples in the dark, as if she had been there before. Dorothy claimed that Sety's ghost visited her and that she had 'been back' to Ancient Egypt in her mind many times. This is how she knew details that baffled experts, she said.

33

Travel tales

Many famous hauntings involve travel of some kind. There are countless tales from all over the world about phantom coaches, cars, trains and buses. Some vehicles seem jinxed, too. Perhaps it's because travel can be dangerous that ghosts and journeys seem so closely linked.

Deathly curse

Princess Amen-Ra died in Egypt over 3,000 years ago. Her body was sealed inside a decorated mummy case. In the 1900s, her tomb was discovered and the mummy case sold to four Englishmen. Within weeks, all four were either dead or terribly ill. When a London museum bought the mummy, anyone who went near it died. A ghost expert warned that the Princess had left a curse on anyone who disturbed her tomb. Unafraid, an American archeologist took it on board the brand new ship, *Titanic*, bound for New York. On the night of April 15, 1912, the ship hit an iceberg and sank, drowning 1,502 people. Nobody mourned the loss of the mummy, which vanished without trace in the icy Atlantic.

Tragic passenger

One story tells of a British Colonel Ewart on his way from Carlisle to London by train in around 1900. Alone in his compartment, the Colonel dozed off. When he woke up, someone had joined him, although it was impossible for anyone to have boarded the train.

A young woman dressed in black was now sitting opposite the Colonel. She sat silently looking down into her lap. Suddenly, the train braked.

A falling suitcase knocked the Colonel out. When he woke up, the woman had gone. But a porter knew who Ewart's silent companion had been.

Years earlier, the woman and her new husband had been on the train. He leaned out of the window, his head was severed and landed in her lap.

Several people 'saw' the *Titanic* sinking in dreams. Others cancelled their tickets on the ship at the last minute - was it just luck or could they foresee something?

Travel tales

On the night of December 28, 1879, a steam train crossing the Tay Bridge in Scotland plunged into the river below. People say that the doomed train still rumbles across the bridge on the same date each year.

In 1865, a train carried the body of Abraham Lincoln, President of the United States, to be buried in Washington. People say they saw the train years later, with a skeleton band playing inside it.

First World War submarine *UB65* seemed jinxed. Some men were killed building it, an officer fell overboard, and one of its own torpedoes killed six of its crew. A ghostly officer was seen on deck just before *UB65* blew up at sea in 1918.

SCOTLAND

New York
Washington

Tay disaster

London
Sarajevo

FRANCE

EGYPT

UB65

Beheaded

R101

Jinx car

Ghost train

Florida

Flight 401

Mummy

PACIFIC OCEAN

ATLANTIC OCEAN

N W E S

In 1972, Flight 401 from New York to Florida crashed, killing 101. Later, crews on Flight 318 said they saw the ghost of the flight engineer of Flight 401. Was it because parts of his plane were used to build theirs?

The airship *R101* crashed in France in 1930. Two days later, its dead captain seemed to 'speak' through a woman named Eileen Garrett. In the captain's voice, she described the crash, in detail only the captain could know.

On June 28, 1914, the Archduke of Austria was shot dead in a red Graf and Sift car in Sarajevo. His death sparked the bloody First World War. Thirteen more deaths were linked with the jinxed car before it was destroyed.

Only the women and children fitted into the *Titanic*'s lifeboats. Most of the men drowned.

Although the night of the disaster was a clear one, the crew did not see the iceberg in time.

35

Tales from the North

Perhaps the ice, snow and long, dark nights in the North are an ideal supernatural setting. In Scandinavia and Russia, tales of sea monsters mingle with those of people with extraordinary powers.

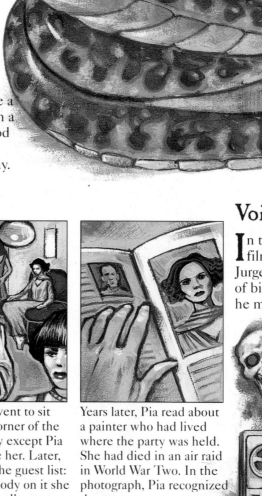

The last sighting of a Lindorn was in the 1930s, but no photographs survive.

Strange creatures

Some of the world's oldest sea monsters are said to inhabit the cold lakes and fjords of Norway. Bronze-age settlers there carved images of giant sea snakes onto their knives more than 3,000 years ago. The strange creatures' heads are more like a horse than a snake, but they slither along like serpents. There are many stories about 'Lindorns', as they are called. Some say they can stride over mountains, others that they capsize boats. One was said to have swallowed cows grazing by a lake.

Fish or man?

Perhaps even odder is the 16th century tale of the Norwegian 'monk-fish'. This sea creature's head looked like a bald medieval monk, with a fleshy hood like the hood on monks' clothes, but with a fish's tail, they say.

Mystery guest

Pia Virtakallio was at a party on February 12, 1977, in Helsinki, Finland, when she saw an older woman in outdated clothes come in from the freezing cold without a coat.

The woman went to sit silently in a corner of the room. Nobody except Pia seemed to see her. Later, Pia checked the guest list: there was nobody on it she didn't know well.

Years later, Pia read about a painter who had lived where the party was held. She had died in an air raid in World War Two. In the photograph, Pia recognized the mystery guest.

Voices from the grave

In the 1950s and '60s, a Swedish film producer, Friedrich Jurgenson, heard faint voices on tapes of birdsong he had made. Fascinated, he made more recordings. The voices said that they were the dead. They spoke in many languages and some even said they had a toothache. They were hard to hear, but some experts really believed they were the dead, others that they were aliens from other planets. Yet others just heard noise.

Strange powers

Some people seem to have the power to contact forces beyond normal life. Are they fakes or truly gifted? See what you make of these.

Burning vision

In September 1759, the Swedish philosopher Emmanuel Swedenborg was with friends in Göteborg, south-west Sweden. Suddenly, he said there was a fire in Stockholm, many hours' journey away, and that his home was in danger. He left, returning later to say that the fire was out - just three doors from his home. Next day, news came of a fire in Stockholm, just as Swedenborg had described it.

Emmanuel Swedenborg

Rasputin

One of the most famous people to claim supernatural powers was a Russian monk called Rasputin. He said he could see the future, perform magic, hypnotize and heal people at will.

The Russian prince, Alexander, suffered from the disease hemophilia, which meant that, if he started to bleed, he could easily bleed to death. In 1905, Alexander fell and began bleeding. Doctors could not save him, but Rasputin swore that he could, saying 'I, Rasputin, have willed it'. The prince survived, and Rasputin became the trusted adviser of the Russian royal family from then on.

Rasputin

Murdered

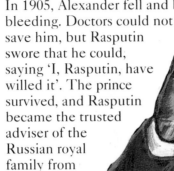

Many people began to envy Rasputin's power and influence. His wild appearance and piercing eyes led some to believe he was mad. In 1916, a group of nobles decided to kill him, but they found the task incredibly difficult. First, they prepared food for Rasputin laced with poison. He ate it, but was unharmed. Then they shot at him, but he managed to run outside. Having beaten him with iron chains, the conspirators tied him up with them and threw him through a hole in the ice on the river Neva. When Rasputin's body was found, he had escaped from his chains and had been trying to claw his way through the ice before he had finally drowned.

Traditionally, in Russia, each October 31st, the spirits of the dead gather for a special church service. Those who have been prayed for by the living can stand behind the altar at the front of the church. Those who have been forgotten stand weeping at the back.

ATLANTIC OCEAN

SWEDEN

FINLAND

Helsinki

NORWAY

Stockholm

Göteborg

NORTH SEA

RUSSIA

River Neva

Moscow

DENMARK

W   E

S

Spirits of Africa and Arabia

In Africa and the Middle East, magic is a living and powerful force to many people. They believe witch doctors can cast spells and banish evil.

Arab stories tell of spirits called genies using magic to grant wishes or inflict curses. Can you think of one in a story that's well-known in the West?

Masters of spells

In many African countries, witch doctors still care for the health of their tribe. The way they diagnose illnesses and the treatments they prescribe may vary from tribe to tribe, but most witch doctors say that illnesses are caused by an evil spirit attacking the victim from within.

Doctor and cure

First, the witch doctor finds out what is wrong by a process called divination. He must follow tribal rituals very carefully. Sometimes the witch doctor consults the position of magic bones or twigs, or he may ask the patient to take part in a sacred ritual as part of the healing process. Cures can include herbal medicines, carefully mixed to treat each specific illness, or the wearing of a special charm or amulet.

Mind power

It is said that the witch doctor has such influence over his African tribespeople because they believe unquestioningly in his powers. Their faith in his abilities cures them or, sometimes, kills them. But can this mind power still work if the victim is not a believing tribe member?

The burglar's revenge

In 1918, in a town in South Africa, on the Basutoland border, a witch doctor was found guilty of burglary and was jailed. Two weeks later, noises were heard in the burgled house as if a large animal was moving around inside it. There was a terrible rumpus in the kitchen as if everything was being thrown about; but when the door was opened, all was exactly as normal.

Old Man Baboon

Locals said the fuss was caused by Old Man Baboon, a spirit sent by the witch doctor to punish them for locking him up. There was no more trouble: maybe the witch doctor felt he was wasting his time trying to scare them.

Genies

In traditional Middle Eastern, or Arab, stories, a Jinni or Djinni appears in many forms. The English word for one of these is a genie; you may have heard of the one that appears in *Aladdin*. A genie can be a good spirit, like a kind of angel, or it can be an evil demon called an Afreet or Ghul.

Stupid spirits

Many Arabic tales tell of genies taking on any shape and moving from place to place in an instant. In *Aladdin*, the good genie shows both its magic power to grant wishes and its traditional stupidity in being tricked into entering a tiny lamp. Evil genies can be kept at bay by reciting words from the Islamic holy text, the Koran.

Genies are also scared of iron and salt, so they say.

Missing bride

Some supernatural stories from Africa and the Middle East deal with more familiar spooky subjects, such as vampires and strange monsters. In one tale, set in Iraq in the 1400s, a wealthy merchant's son called Abul-Hassain fell in love with a beautiful young woman called Nadilla. They were married in the city of Baghdad, but Hassain grew puzzled by his wife's habits.

Nadilla never ate at home. She also left their bed as soon as she thought Hassain was asleep and only returned an hour before dawn. One night, Hassain rose and secretly followed Nadilla. She went to the city cemetary, to a large tomb.

Hassain crept up to spy on her and recoiled in horror. He saw people devouring the flesh of long-dead corpses. Hassain ran home, but said nothing. When Nadilla again refused to eat he said that he knew what kind of flesh she preferred.

Nadilla did not speak, but crept silently to bed. When Hassain joined her, she tore at his throat and tried to drink his blood, before fleeing. Hassain pursued her to the tomb and there burned her to ashes: it was the only way to end his torment.

Dead or alive?

Intriguing tales of monsters stem from the remote swamps of Central Africa. In 1913, a European-led expedition reported a big, pale brown animal the size of an elephant, browsing in the swamps around the Sanga River. It had a long, smooth neck and one extra-long tooth at the front.

Dark secrets

A zoologist and explorer, Ivan T. Sanderson, encountered a similar creature on a different river in 1932. It burst from a riverside cave as his canoe passed, plunged into the water and disappeared. His African guides shouted M'koo-m'bemboo and fled in terror. European experts then called the monster the Mokele-mbembe.

Many locals said they had seen the creatures. An old man called Firman Mosomole picked it out immediately when shown pictures of dinosaurs in a book. An expert said it certainly sounded like a dinosaur when he interviewed witnesses.

More mysteries

For decades, expeditions hunted the living dinosaurs. One American institute even offered a huge reward for anyone who could find one, dead or alive. Nobody has ever claimed it.

Australia and New Zealand

For thousands of years, the Aboriginal and Maori peoples roamed Australia and New Zealand, telling tales of strange monsters and powerful spirits. When European settlers arrived in the 1700s, their ideas about ghosts were altogether different.

The Bunyip

The Aboriginal people warned early European settlers about the Bunyip. Some described it as like a flabby beast with the head of a cow, others as a huge pig with a striped body. All agreed that the Bunyip trapped victims by making them feel cold and powerless to escape. The Bunyip is supposed to lurk in the deep, dirty water in Australia's swamps. It slithers out of the murky depths, makes a noise like a child moaning, then silently drags its prey to a watery death.

Sacred places

The Aboriginal people believe that some places are full of evil, others of good. They see the land as a song, crossed by sacred paths called 'dream lines', or 'song lines'. They tell stories of 'The Dreaming', when their world was created.

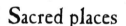

Aboriginal art shows their belief in the importance of all living things.

Corroborees

Some places in Australia, such as the famous landmark Ayers Rock, are especially sacred for the Aboriginal people. Religious ceremonies called corroborees were held here, as well as at another sacred place called Corroboree Rock.

In 1959, a clergyman visited Corroboree Rock. Thinking himself alone, he took a photograph. When it was developed, a shadowy figure could be seen emerging from the bush. Nobody has ever found out who it could be.

Powerful magic

Aboriginal witch doctors, called Kurdaitcha, wield great power. If one points a 'pointing-bone' at someone, for instance, the victim believes a splinter pierces his soul and kills him. In 1956, an Aboriginal boy was flown to a Darwin hospital. He almost died, saying a Kurdaitcha had 'pointed the bone' at him. Doctors were powerless to help and he only recovered when his people told him that the curse was lifted.

Maori rules

The Maori people of New Zealand also lived by rules called 'tapus', or taboos. Their chief priests, or tohungas, enforced them. 'Supernatural' punishment followed any law-breaking.

AUSTRALIA
Corroboree Rock
Alice Springs
Ayers Rock
Murray River
Sydney
Albury
Melbourne

NEW ZEALAND

Maoris carved totem poles like this to ward off evil.

Settlers' ghosts

Settlers' ghost stories are more familiar to most than the magic of the tribal peoples. In these two, ghosts seem to have a good reason for haunting a world they have left.

In 1826, a farmer called Fred Fisher disappeared on the road from Sydney to Melbourne. No trace of him was found, but people began to see a mysterious man on a bridge above a creek on Fisher's route. He was pale, witnesses said, and seemed to point to a spot far below him.

Detective work

As reports of the strange figure grew, police decided to dig up the spot the man had pointed to. They found the bones of Fred Fisher, who had been murdered and buried there. The culprit was found and punished and the ghost disappeared forever.

The lonely place Fisher haunted is now called Fisher's Ghost Creek.

Too late

An Australian farmer named Brown was taking cattle to market near Albury. As he slept that night at an inn, he awoke to see his wife there, urgently beckoning.

Brown asked the landlord if he had seen a woman arrive, but he had seen nobody. Puzzled and worried, Brown rode home as fast as he could. Could he have had a nightmare?

As he approached his farm near the Murray River, some friends stopped his horse and took Brown quietly to one side. The news they had to tell him was horrifying indeed.

Brown heard that a servant had killed his wife, angry at her cruel treatment. She had died at the exact hour that her spirit had materialized next to his bed, far away.

Royal and famous ghosts

Powerful people often lead dramatic, extraordinary lives. Many of them also meet sudden and violent deaths. Perhaps it is the deep impression they make on the world during their life that makes their ghosts linger on, unwilling to leave it.

Royal legend

Weaving a web of sorcery, bravery and fierce loyalty, the tales of King Arthur, the magician Merlin and the knights of the Round Table have enchanted people for centuries. Mystery surrounds Arthur's death in the 6th century, and his burial place.

According to legend, he is not dead, but 'sleeping' on the magical Isle of Avalon, said to be on the site of Glastonbury town, and he will wake to lead his people again.

Sacred site

The Holy Grail, the cup used by Jesus Christ at his last supper before his arrest and crucifixion, is also said to be at the bottom of a well in Glastonbury, called Chalice Well. Arthur's trusty knights were sent to find the Grail, but only Sir Galahad saw it.

King Arthur and his ghostly knights are said to charge down Cadbury Hill, near Glastonbury, each Midsummer's Day.

The mist-shrouded Tor that overlooks the town of Glastonbury is claimed to be the site of the palace of Gwyn ap Nudd, King of the Fairies. Some say the stone tower that tops the summit of the Tor hides an entrance to the magical 'underworld'.

Men of power

Not the ghost of a king, but that of a president stalks the corridors of the White House, in Washington DC, USA. Although the spirits of several American presidents have been seen in there, the most frequent phantom visitor is the great Abraham Lincoln, shot dead in 1865. His grim-faced ghost has been seen in the Blue Room, the Lincoln Room, the Rose Room, the East Room and the Oval Room.

Shocking sight

Among the many accounts of the ghost is that of a servant, Mary Eban, who was cleaning the Lincoln Room one day. She looked up to see Lincoln's spirit sitting on a chair, pulling off his boots. Another story features Queen Wilhelmina of the Netherlands, who was staying at the White House in 1943. One night, someone knocked at her bedroom door. She told them to enter, but nobody did. When the queen opened it, she saw the ghost of Lincoln silently standing in the hall in a black top hat. She fainted with shock, though her host, President Roosevelt, was not at all surprised to hear what she had seen.

Strange visitor

French Emperor, Napoleon Bonaparte, held great power during his life. By 1821, his military and political ambitions in ruins, he was exiled to the remote island of St. Helena.

On May 5, Napoleon's mother received a tall, male visitor at her home in Rome. He wore a wide hat, masking his face, and a flowing, dark cloak. He insisted he could speak only to Madame Bonaparte.

Softly, the man told her that her son had died that day. She was shocked and puzzled - news took weeks to come from St. Helena; and, just as troubling, she felt sure she had seen her visitor somewhere before.

Over two months later, Madame Bonaparte heard that her son, Napoleon, had indeed died on May 5. Only then did she realize that her son's spirit must have visited her on the day of his death.

Rule of blood

Perhaps even more powerful than Napoleon, and almost certainly more ruthless, Henry VIII ruled England in the 1500s with little pity. Anyone who displeased him was executed, whatever their rank.

Bloody horror

One of the most gruesome famous hauntings concerns the execution of Margaret, Countess of Salisbury, in 1541. Even though she was over seventy, she had a claim to the throne, so Henry VIII ordered her death.

The Countess said that she had committed no crime and refused to put her head on the block. The blindfolded executioner then chased her around the room, hacking clumsily at her as he went. This ghastly scene is replayed each year in the Tower of London, on the sad anniversary of the Countess's messy death.

Unlucky queens

Hampton Court Palace, just outside London, throngs with ghosts from Henry's reign. The most frequent sad visitors are three of his seven wives: Anne Boleyn and Catherine Howard died on the block; while Jane Seymour, his third wife, though spared her head, died twelve days after the birth of Henry's long-awaited son, Edward.

The spirit of Anne Boleyn glides through the palace's rooms and grounds.

Washington

Cadbury Hill

Glastonbury

Hampton Court Palace, near London

Rome

St. Helena

Jane Seymour's sad ghost haunts Hampton Court, dressed in white and carrying a lighted candle.

Imprisoned at Hampton Court before her death, Catherine Howard ran one night to the palace Chapel to beg Henry for her life. Her ghost still makes this last, hopeless run.

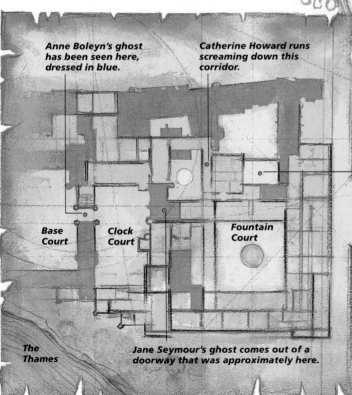

Anne Boleyn's ghost has been seen here, dressed in blue.

Catherine Howard runs screaming down this corridor.

Henry's ghost is still seen in the Chapel.

Base Court

Clock Court

Fountain Court

The Thames

Jane Seymour's ghost comes out of a doorway that was approximately here.

43

Ghosts in film and fiction

Most people have seen a ghost, in a play or film, or on television. Spooky stories have had willing readers for centuries, too. Perhaps we feel safe meeting ghosts in 'unreal' situations?

Stage spooks

Theatrical ghosts in plays give us a thrill of terror, but also allow us to face our fears of the supernatural.

Shakespeare's ghosts

One of the world's most famous playwrights, William Shakespeare, used ghosts to chill audiences in several of his plays.
In *Richard III*, the pitiful ghosts of two boy princes (see page 5) appear to King Richard, who murdered them earlier in the play. In *Julius Caesar*, Caesar's ghost appears to remind one of his slayers, Brutus, of his crime. In *The Winter's Tale*, dead Queen Hermione returns to life at the end of the play.
In *Hamlet*, the ghost of Prince Hamlet's father appears to accuse Hamlet's uncle, Claudius, of murdering him.

Spooky banquet

Perhaps the most chilling of all the ghosts in Shakespeare's plays appears in *Macbeth*. Having murdered King Duncan and crowned himself, Macbeth is holding a banquet to celebrate. As the guests sit down, the ghost of a noble called Banquo - also murdered by Macbeth - sits down too. The other diners watch in amazement as tough Macbeth is terrified by something he says he can see in what seems to be an empty chair. In some productions of the play the actor playing Banquo sits at the table, looking suitably ghoulish. In others, people are asked to imagine him.

Macbeth's celebration banquet turns into a nightmare when the murderer sees Banquo's ghost sit in the chair he had reserved for himself.

A Christmas Carol

In the 1800s, a ghastly ghost gripped readers of Charles Dickens' story, *A Christmas Carol*. In it, miserly Ebeneezer Scrooge receives a warning he cannot ignore from the ghost of his dead partner, Jacob Marley.

Beware!

Marley's ghost warns Scrooge of the miserable fate that awaits him if he does not treat others with more kindness. He ushers in three other ghosts to visit a terrified Scrooge. They teach him a lesson which is enough to make him change his ways.

The first ghostly guest is the joyful ghost of his childhood Christmases.

Next comes the lonely, miserable spirit of his present Christmas.

The grisly 'ghost of Christmas future' shows people glad at his death.

Movie monsters

The horror movie business really took off in the 1930s, when filmgoers discovered the thrill of being scared. Two of the earliest horror movies are classics today, though they probably don't scare today's sophisticated audiences. They are *Frankenstein* and *Dracula*.

Monstrous tale

The story of Frankenstein was written by a young woman called Mary Shelley. On a trip to Switzerland with her poet husband, Percy B. Shelley and his friend, the poet Byron in 1818, each dared the others to write a 'monstrous... horrendous' story. One night, Mary had a dream about a man creating a monster from parts of dead bodies. This horrible dream inspired her to write *Frankenstein*. The book was filmed in 1931, starring Boris Karloff.

Boris Karloff as the monster in the dungeon scene from *Frankenstein*.

It was seen as so shocking that some scenes were cut before audiences saw it. One of these showed the monster throwing a little girl into a lake, where, of course, she does not float. The story was filmed again in 1994, in a version based closely on Mary Shelley's novel. It starred Robert de Niro as the monstrous creature.

Bloodsucker

Bram Stoker's novel, *Count Dracula*, was first filmed as a black and white movie called *Dracula* in 1931. It starred a Romanian actor called Bela Lugosi who played the role of Dracula so many times that he was buried in Dracula's black cloak lined with red satin when he died.

Bela Legosi as Dracula.

In 1958, the British film company, Hammer House of Horror filmed the story of *Count Dracula*, starring the actor Christopher Lee as the bloodthirsty vampire Count. Lee's saturnine good looks and chilling quest for blood enthralled and repelled audiences everywhere.

Christopher Lee and Melissa Stribling in the 1958 Hammer production of Dracula.

Horrors of today

Recent films have combined suspense with vivid special effects to horrify and excite audiences even more. In 1979, the grisly story of the evil at work in a house in Amityville, USA (see page 4) was brought to life in a successful film. The 1982 film *Poltergeist* told the tale of a family reduced to terror by a poltergeist that seemed to speak through their television. The being took possession of a young girl, leading to some nail-bitingly tense scenes.

A scene from *Poltergeist* featuring Jobeth Williams.

Many films focus on supernatural phenomena such as UFOs, possession by evil spirits and the dead returning to life as living dead, or zombies. Some of these are badly-made, but others, such as *The Exorcist* in 1973, made film history in their use of stunning special effects. With its cast of bungling amateur ghost hunters, the 1984 film *Ghostbusters* was a huge hit. Although it was a comedy, at its heart was the message that all around us, wherever we are, ghosts may lurk.

This is the *Ghostbusters* film logo.

Talking to ghosts

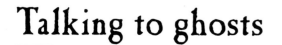

In most ghost stories, phantoms haunt this world. But some people claim that they can get in touch with ghosts in their world, beyond death. Whether you believe their claims or not, they are hard to ignore.

Ghostly voices?

In the West, people called mediums claim they can talk to ghosts, and have other powers too. During the 1900s, contacting dead friends and relatives at meetings called seances was particularly popular. At a seance, a medium goes into a deep sleep called a trance before 'communicating with the spirits' and passing on their messages. Some mediums are frauds, using tricks to make money out of people's longing to talk to their dead loved ones. Others may not be....

CANADA

ICELAND

POLAND

NORTH AMERICA

GERMANY

JAPAN

SOUTH AMERICA

BRAZIL

Sao Paolo

People often touched hands and waited for a spirit to communicate through the medium at a seance.

Indridi Indridason

Indridi Indridason was an Icelandic medium with astounding powers. In 1908, a scientist searched him, wrapped him in a net and held his hands as he went into a trance. Heavy objects flew around, unseen hands played a music box and Indridason rose into the air. The scientist was unable to prove any trickery.

Stefan Ossowiecki

Stefan Ossowiecki became famous in Poland in the 1920s and 30s. He could 'read' messages that were inside sealed envelopes. Nobody ever managed to prove him a fraud.

Willy Schneider

Willy Schneider, who lived in Germany in the 1920s, also made things rise into the air while people were holding his hands. He could make handkerchiefs move as if invisible hands were inside them while his own hands and feet were bound.

Mirabelli

The medium Carlos Mirabelli was born near Sao Paolo, Brazil, in 1889. He claimed he could make objects float around, and rise into the air himself, or levitate.

This photograph claims to prove that Mirabelli could levitate.

Miraculous?

Perhaps most amazing of all, Mirabelli claimed that he could make dead people reappear at seances. When one dead man 'materialized', doctors examined him and declared him a real person. When he began to vanish before their eyes, one doctor touched him and described feeling just 'a spongy mass'. The experts were unable to prove Mirabelli was a fraud.

Houdini's hunt

Mina Crandon, an American medium during the early 1900s, called herself 'Margery' and claimed that her dead brother, Walter, helped her move things without touching them, and contact the spirits of the dead. Her claims angered the escape artist, Harry Houdini, who decided to prove that 'Margery' was a fraud.

Box of tricks

Houdini locked the medium inside a wooden box so that only her head and hands stuck out. As the seance began, the box burst open - Margery said 'Walter' was very angry. When she was shut into it again, something inside shook and banged so much that the experiment had to be abandoned. Houdini was left frustrated.

Houdini in the box he put Margery Crandon into to try to prove her a fake.

Ghost power

People around the world believe that the spirits of the dead watch over their families and have a part to play in their lives. In Japan, people called 'mikos' claim to summon ghosts to meetings. Speaking through the miko, the ghost usually talks to each family member in turn, before returning to the world of the dead. Some of these reunions last for several hours.

The Shaking Tent

In Canadian Indian communities, men called 'pilotois' say they talk to ghosts in a ritual called 'The Shaking Tent'. The pilotois goes into a wigwam alone and creates such supernatural power that, not only can he be heard talking to 'someone' inside, but the wigwam shakes, lights up and lifts into the air.

Days for the Dead

In South America, people believe that the spirits of the dead visit Earth on the first two days of November to enjoy themselves. These days are called 'Todos Santos' (All Saints), or 'The Days of the Dead'. 'Todos Santos' is not sad; it's a huge celebration.

A feast of special food is laid out by each family for the ghosts to enjoy. People make masks and models of skeletons and talk about their memories of dead loved ones. Children are sometimes given skulls made of sugar crystal, too. People feel it is a time to welcome ghosts, not fear them.

There is a picture of the dead relative.

Skulls made of sugar crystal, papier mâché and pottery

Candles
Cempasuchil flowers

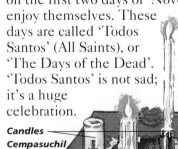

© Mary Evans / Guy Playfair

© Mary Evans / Harry Price Coll., Univ. of London

Glossary of the supernatural

Abominable snowman: huge, legendary ape-like creature, said to inhabit the Himalayan mountains. Also called a Yet-Teh or Yeti. **See page 30.**

Banshee: Irish female spirit who weeps, howls and screams. She usually appears to warn people that one of their family is going to die. **See page 9.**

Black dog: phantom animal in stories from many countries. In Britain often called Black Shuck. It can have one blazing eye, paws pointing the wrong way or no head. **See page 10.**

Bunyip: legendary monster said to inhabit swamps and lagoons in Australia. **See page 40.**

Ch'iang Shich: sort of vampire in ghost stories from China. **See page 27.**

Curse of the Pharaohs: Ancient Egyptian message at the entrance to Tutankhamun's tomb. **See page 32.**

Devil: chief spirit of evil. Often depicted in the West as a human-like figure with horns, cloven hoofs and a tail. **See pages 6, 20.**

Fakir: men from India who train their minds with physical and mental exercises called yoga. They can overcome pain and even cheat death. **See page 30.**

Genie: magical spirits in stories from the Middle East. Genies appear by magic and sometimes fulfil a person's wishes. Also called Afreet, Djinni or Jinni. **See pages 3, 38.**

Ghost: the supernatural presence of something or someone from the past or present. **See pages 5, 43.**

Ghoul: a mean and evil-looking spirit or ghost, said to feed on the dead. **See pages 8, 12, 44.**

Kattidya: a type of witch in Indian stories. **See page 31.**

Kurdaitcha: Aboriginal witch doctor, who appears to possess magical powers. **See page 40.**

Lindorn: legendary sea snakes, said to inhabit the cold lakes and fjords of Norway. **See pages 3, 36.**

Lung meis: unseen 'dragon paths', running underground between hill-tops across China. **See page 26.**

Medium: person said to have psychic powers that enable him or her to talk to the dead and to receive their messages. **See page 46.**

Mikos: people from Japan, who claim they can summon ghosts to family meetings. **See page 47.**

Mokele-mbembe: a monster, said to inhabit rivers in Africa. It is supposed to look like a dinosaur. **See page 39.**

Nagual: spirit companion bird or animal, once believed by Aztec Indians in Central America to fight alongside their warriors in battles. **See page 29.**

Phantom: another term for a ghost.

Poltergeist: noisy, mischievous spirits. They can move objects through the air and cause physical damage. **See page 21.**

Seance: a meeting at which a medium (see above) attempts to receive messages from the spirits of the dead. **See pages 46, 47.**

Shamans: tribal priests. People say they can communicate with spirits, look into the future and cure diseases. **See page 14.**

Spirit: the soul of a person, believed to survive after the body dies. It cannot be touched or seen. Many people think the soul passes into an afterlife and can contact the living, although it does not haunt the Earth. **See pages 12, 45, 47.**

Spook: another word for ghost. **See pages 4, 5, 6, 44.**

Tulpas: according to Tibetan belief, spirits brought to 'life' by intense meditation. **See page 30.**

U.F.O.s: Unidentified Flying Objects such as flying saucers. **See pages 2, 14, 45.**

Vampire: dead person, supposed to rise from the grave to drink the blood of the living. This term is also sometimes applied to strange, blood-sucking animals. If bitten by a vampire, the victim is transformed into one too, and is extremely difficult to kill. **See pages 18-19, 39.**

Werewolves: people who are transformed into wolves at every full moon, when they kill and devour humans. Other animals feature in similar stories from all over the world. **See page 11.**

Witch: in folk tales a person, normally female, who practises magic or sorcery, or is believed to have dealings with the devil. **See page 11.**

Zombie: corpse brought back to life by a sorceror using witchcraft in the Caribbean. **See pages 2, 14, 45.**

Haunted places

Abbey of Iona: Scotland. Burned and robbed during a Viking raid in the 10th century. **See page 28.**

Ayers Rock: Australia. Famous landmark, where Aboriginals held religious ceremonies. **See page 40.**

Bermuda Triangle: an area in the Atlantic Ocean between Bermuda, Florida and Puerto Rico, where many have disappeared forever. **See page 25.**

Bettiscombe Manor: England. The skull of a former slave is kept here, to appease an angry ghost. **See page 9.**

Bisham Abbey: England. The ghost of Dame Elizabeth Hoby mourns the death of her son here. **See page 6.**

Borley Rectory: England. Most haunted house. **See page 6.**

Bran castle: Romania. Home of Vlad the Impaler. **See page 18.**

Eilean Mór lighthouse: off the west coast of Scotland. Three lighthouse keepers mysteriously vanished from here. **See page 25.**

Fisher's Ghost Creek: Australia. Bridge above a creek, haunted by the ghost of Fred Fisher. **See page 41.**

Glamis Castle: Scotland. Haunted for centuries by a monstrous baby and other supernatural beings. **See page 6.**

Great Pyramid of King Cheops: Gizah, Egypt. Largest pyramid ever built and the oldest of the Seven Wonders of the World. **See page 32.**

Hampton Court: palace on the Thames, near London. Haunted by many ghosts from Henry VIII's reign. **See page 43.**

Littlecote House: near Hungerford, England. Home of murder suspect 'Wild William'. **See page 22.**

Petit Trianon: Versailles, France. Part of the Palace of King Louis XIV, where two women claim to have travelled back in time. **See page 21.**

Silver Cliff : Colorado, USA. A town famous for its 'dancing blue spirits'. **See page 12.**

Tower of London: by the Thames in London. Prison where many gruesome deaths took place. **See page 5.**

Wartburg castle: Eisenach, Germany. Hiding place of Martin Luther during the 1500s. **See page 20.**

Winchester Mystery House: California, USA. Sara Winchester claimed she was compelled to build this house by spirits. **See page 7.**

First published in 1995 by Usborne Publishing Ltd, 83-85 Saffron Hill, London EC1N 8RT, England. Copyright © Usborne Publishing Ltd, 1995.